The Book of Kisses

For Ray—

Hope this offers you a few
practical tips for use out there
in the field.
Happy kissing!
All best,
Danny. 12/84

DANNY BIEDERMAN

The Book of Kisses

DEMBNER BOOKS
NEW YORK

Dembner Books
Published by Red Dembner Enterprises Corp., 1841 Broadway, New York, N.Y. 10023
Distributed by W. W. Norton & Company, Inc., 500 Fifth Avenue, New York, N.Y. 10110

Library of Congress Cataloging in Publication Data

Biederman, Danny.
 The book of kisses.

 1. Kissing. 2. Kissing in literature.
I. Title.
GT2640.B54   1984   394   84-7667
ISBN 0-934878-42-0 (pbk.)

Dedication

Here's to the smoke that curls in the air
  Here's to the dog at my feet;
Here's to the girls that have gone before,—
  Gad! but their kisses were sweet!

                               —Anonymous

"May I print a kiss on your lips?" I said,
  And she nodded her full permission;
So we went to press and I rather guess
  We printed a full edition.

             —Joseph Lilienthal, "A Full Edition"

To Bea, the sweetest of them all, and the lady who—by way of the volumes *we've* printed together—was my loving inspiration for this very special edition.

Kisses of Gratitude

I would like to extend my gratitude to the following people for their individual contributions. Thanks go to

My parents, Harry and Esther, for three decades of constant giving of themselves—more love and support than any son could ever hope for. Jerry and Debbie, faithful brother and sister, for their longtime love and support, plus professional advice relating to, respectively, the publishing and music fields. Corky, a truly prolific kisser and my best buddy, for always being there with plenty of love through all the ups and downs and life.

Beatríz Máynez, for twelve years of yum—and for her frequent application of the Hindu *Chalitaka*, the kiss that a woman bestows on her man while he is "absorbed in an artistic pursuit."

Irving and Sylvia Wallace, David, Flora and Eli Wallechinsky, Amy and Josef Mark—for their advice, valuable contributions, and the great opportunity to work with and learn from all of them. Marie Piscitello, for her close friendship these many years, and for the hard work she so graciously and professionally contributed toward this book. Carol Orsag Madigan, for her expert advice, contributions, and friendship. Paul Surratt, Steve Dworman, Mell Lazarus, Robert Short, Linda Brevelle, and Mike Lefebvre for their very thoughtful contributions. The staff of the Margaret Herrick Library for their professional and indispensable research assistance.

Maria Carvainis, for her great belief in this book and her many efforts on its behalf.

Dr. Michael Hall and the Jules Stein Eye Institute, for whom I worked in 1972 when, over racks of test tubes and radioactive waste, the idea for this book was born.

Additional thanks for their continued support go to the Great Mujumbo and Mrs. Mu, the Kaufman family, the Máynez family, Stan, Norm, Jeff and the entire crew of Stan's Corner Donut Shoppe of Westwood, California, Sam Rolfe, Chris Soldo, as well as, in memory, grandparents Mae and Bessie and Alex, and finally, all those wonderful ladies in the field who, over the years, have provided so much valuable research *and* continued incentive.

D. B.

Contents

Why a Kiss?

 ## 1. What Is a Kiss?

What is a kiss? Is it not a fervent attempt to absorb, to breathe in, a portion of the being whom we love?

—Giovanni Jacopo Casanova

Trivia Question

An ancient name for what is ever new though ten thousand times repeated.

—Frederick Greenwood, *The Lover's Lexicon*

Medically Speaking

A contraction of the mouth due to an enlargement of the heart.

—Anonymous

Grammatically Speaking

It is a noun both common and proper,
Not very singular, and agrees with both *you* and *me*.

—Anonymous

The Kiss Circumstantial

A kiss is a peculiar proposition. Of no use to one, yet absolute bliss to two. The small boy gets it for nothing, the young man has to steal it, and the old man has to buy it. The Baby's right, the Lover's privilege, the Hypocrite's mask. To a young girl, faith; to a married woman, hope; to an old maid, charity.

—Anonymous

Broad View

The pressure of the mouth on a body.
—*Dictionary of the Scientific Associations*

The Doctor's Definition

A caress given with the lips.
—Dr. Hugo C. Beigel

Let's Flex

The anatomical juxtaposition of two orbicularis oris muscles in a state of contraction.
—Dr. Henry Gibbons, "Definition of a Kiss"

So Much for Romance

A bite and a suction.
—P. d'Enjoy

Kiss as Metaphor

The kiss . . . is not to be referred to the bite, or even to gustation, much less to mastication, suction, or olfactory processes. The primary movement of the lips is simply transferred to a metaphorical use, so to say, and their sensitiveness is applied to a secondary object, whose stimulus is not hunger, but the analogous emotion of love, affection, and veneration.

—Ernest Crawley, *The Mystic Rose*

Holberg's Absolutism

A kiss is only a salutation, and cannot be considered otherwise.

—Ludvig Holberg

Ah, More!

What's in a kiss?
Oh, when for love the kiss is given, this:
Truth, purity, abiding trust, the seal
Of loyalty to love, come woe, come weal,
Unspoken promise of a soul's allegiance—this,
All this, and more, ah more! is in a kiss.

—Marion Phelps, "What's in a Kiss?"

Where There's a Bill, There's a Way

John Henry's Best

Is not a kiss the very autograph of love?
                    —Henry T. Finck
                    Romantic Love and Personal Beauty

Even-Steven

That which you cannot give without taking and cannot take without
giving.

                    —Anonymous

A Sticky Situation

What is a kiss? Why this, as some approve:
The sure sweet cement, glue, and lime of love.
                    —Robert Herrick, "A Kiss"

And Three's a Crowd

A pleasant reminder that two heads are better than one.
                    —Rex Prouty

Next to a Hot Fudge Sundae

A kiss is one of the most potent stimulants that a man or woman can
indulge in.

                    —Sheikh Nefzawi, *The Perfumed Garden*

Going Down?

What is a kiss? An inquiry on the second floor as to whether the first floor
is free.

                    —Art Garfunkel to a team of psychologists
                    Bad Timing: A Sensual Obsession (World Northal, 1980)

All in the Family

Kissing is nigh parent and cousin unto the foul feat or deed.

—*The Book of the Knight of La Tour-Landry*, 1372

Open Kiss-a-Me

The Key to Paradise, the blossom of love.

—Definition attributed to an ancient Greek poet

The Setup

Something that often leads to marriage because it leaves something to be desired.

—Definition adapted from Robert Fontaine

Soul'd Out

The seal with which lovers plight their troth—a symbol of the union of souls.

—Konrad Burdach

The Kiss Speaketh

I am just two and two, I am warm, I am cold,
And the parents of numbers that cannot be told,
I am lawful, unlawful—a duty, a fault—
I am often sold dear, good for nothing when bought;
An extraordinary boon, and a matter of course,
And yielded with pleasure when taken by force.

—William Cowper

Between You and Me

A secret told to the mouth instead of the ear.

—Edmond Rostand

Parlez-Vous Baiser?

Kissing . . . is of so much significance that it may be regarded, if not as a separate language of Love, at least as a special dialect—perhaps the long-sought world language intelligible to all?

—Henry T. Finck
Romantic Love and Personal Beauty

Check Your Soup

A kiss is the twenty-seventh letter of the alphabet . . . the love-labial which it takes two to speak plainly.

—Oliver Wendell Holmes

A Romantic Gauge

A kiss can be a comma, a question mark, or an exclamation point. That's basic spelling that every woman ought to know.

—Mistinguette (Jeanne-Marie Bourgeois)

Tongue-Tied

A course of procedure, cunningly devised, for the mutual stoppage of speech at a moment when words are superfluous.

—Oliver Herford

The General Wouldn't Have Liked It

A salute by tasting.

—Sir E. B. Tylor, British anthropologist

Stir Together and Bring to a Boil

Here's to four sweet lips, two pure souls and one undying affection,—love's pretty ingredients for a kiss.

—Christian Nestell Bovee

Kissing—Is it "the long-sought word language intelligible to all"?

No Preservatives Added

Something made of nothing, tasting very sweet,
A most delicious compound, with ingredients complete;
But if, as on occasion, the heart and mind are sour,
It has no great significance, and loses half its power.
> —Mary E. Buell, "The Kiss"

Bottoms Up

What is a kiss? Alacke! at worst,
A single Dropp to quenche a Thirst,
Tho' oft it prooves, in happie Hour,
The first swete Dropp of our long showre.
> —Charles Godfrey Leland, *In the Old Time*

Pour Me Another

A delightful and invigorating beverage . . . it iz nectar for the gods.
> —Josh Billings (Henry Wheeler Shaw), "Kissing"

Momma

So There!

A kiss is a grain of matter to be washed out by any one who wants it.

—Anonymous

But What Is It, *Really?*

When all is said, what is a kiss? An oath of allegiance taken in closer proximity, a promise more precise, a seal on a confession, a rose-red dot upon the letter "i" in loving; a secret which elects the mouth for ear; an instant of eternity murmuring like a bee; a balmy communion with a flower of flowers; a fashion of inhaling each other's heart, and of tasting, on the brink of lips, each other's soul!

—Edmond Rostand, *Cyrano de Bergerac*

Down-Home Advice

The only way tew deskribe a kiss is tew take one, and then set down, awl alone, out of the draft, and smack yure lips.

—Josh Billings, "Kissing"

By Mell Lazarus

—— 17 ——

2. Whose Idea, Anyway?

Lord! I wonder what fool it was that first invented kissing.
—Jonathan Swift

The Adam Theory

1. Nature was its author, and it began with the first courtship.
—Richard Steele

2. If you sarch the rekords ever so lively yu kan't find the author of the first kiss; kissing, like mutch other good things, is ananymous.

But there iz sitch natur in it, sitch a world ov language without words, sitch a heap ov pathos without fuss, so mutch honey, and so little water, so cheap, so sudden, and so neat a mode of striking up an acquaintance that I consider it a good purchase that Adam giv, and got, the fust kiss.

Who kan imagin a grater lump of earthly bliss, reduced tew a finer thing, than kissing the only woman on earth in the garden of Eden.

Adam wasn't the man, I don't beleave, tew pass sich a hand.

I may be wrong in mi konklusions, but if enny body kan date kissing further back i would like tew see them do it.
—Josh Billings, "Kissing"

Traced to an Angel

[The kiss is] as old as creation, and yet as young and fresh as ever. It pre-existed, still exists, and always will exist. Depend upon it, Eve learned it in Paradise, and was taught its beauties, virtues, and varieties by an angel, there is something so transcendent in it.
—Richard Halliburton

Monkey Business

Henry T. Finck has claimed in *Romantic Love and Personal Beauty* that "the Chimpanzee seems to have been the first who discovered the charm of mutual labial contact." He cited a letter received from a Mr. Bartlett that described two chimps who "sat opposite, touching each other with their much-protruded lips." Additionally, Finck noted that in the January 1885 issue of the *Journal of Comparative Medicine and Surgery*, Dr. C. Pitfield Mitchell published these observations of a chimp in New York's Central Park:

"That tender emotions are experienced may be inferred from the fact that [the chimp] pressed the kitten to his breast and kissed it, holding it very gently in both hands. In kissing, the lips are pouted and the tongue protruded, and both are pressed upon the object of affection."

In *Patterns of Sexual Behavior*, authors Clellan S. Ford and Frank A. Beach reported that "when immature male and female chimpanzees are playing they occasionally press their mouths together. . . ." The authors cited a 1914 study in which "the female [ape] seemed to invite contact with [the male's] mouth, for she persistently thrust her smacking lips towards the male, until he . . . touched her lips with his own."

In a 1973 article titled "Communication of Sexual Interest," Dr. Gordon W. Hewes stated flatly: "Apes kiss . . . as a demonstrative, affectionate greeting."

How Irrigating

He is good to kiss for thirst.

—Anonymous

Self-Defeating Solution

The Farmer's Almanac suggests that, ironically, kissing was actually a by-product of man's desire to cool off. The cooling chemical effect of salt consumption on the human body was found to be advantageous on hot days, and one convenient source of salt was the skin of another person. Voila!

The Way to a Man's Heart

1. She threw herself on Kamar-al-Zaman and kissed him on the mouth like a pigeon feeding its young.

—Sir Richard Burton, *Thousand Nights*

2. Kissing may be an adult modification of the instinctive infantile yearning to nurse on mother's nipple. An even more obvious origin is

mouth-to-mouth feeding—the process whereby the mother predigests the food in her own body prior to regurgitating and transferring it into the mouths of her young. It is a custom practiced in many cultures, and is common among many animal species.

Either way, hunger and affection become intertwined at birth, perhaps laying the physiological and emotional groundwork for our later, oft-felt desire to "devour" or "eat up" the one we love.

Of course, other species—such as some female snakes and black widow spiders—*do* consume their mates. The relationship among kissing, eating, and mating seems to fit neatly into the cyclical order of the universe, and is in fact reinforced by a study of other life forms.

In a species of Australian frog, infants enter the world via their mother's mouth. The mother swallows her fertilized eggs, allowing tadpoles to hatch and grow in her stomach until they become frogs, whereupon they emerge. Termites consume a contraceptive secretion provided by their queen that secures her reign until she becomes sterile and is at once devoured by her colony. And the male sciomyzid fly produces a white, frothy food from his mouth for the female, a clever diversion which allows him to have his way with her once she's sat down to chow.

Kissing may be a direct by-product of infantile nursing, but in the overall picture, it is only one elemental variation found within the ever-continuing process of birth and death.

Freudian Lip

The kiss . . . between the mucous membranes of the lips of the two people concerned, is held in high sexual esteem among many nations (including the most highly civilized ones) in spite of the fact that the parts of the body involved do not form part of the sexual apparatus but constitute the entrance to the digestive tract.

—Attributed to Sigmund Freud

Love's Appetite

Lips, however rosy, must be fed.

—Anonymous

The Wild, Wild West

The contact of the lips in the kiss is an inspired discovery and development of the Western World. Strange as it may seem . . . the kiss was unknown in many parts of the world until Western explorers, traders and missionaries carried their customs to the remote parts of our planet.

—William Fielding
Strange Customs of Courtship and Marriage

British Import

The stately visit of a foreign princess was responsible for introducing the kiss to England, according to a report in an 1871 issue of the *St. James Gazette*, which quoted royal Friesland historian Saint Pierius Wensemius. In a 1622 article which appeared in his publication *Chronicle*, Wensemius claimed that kissing was "unpractised and unknown in England till the fair Princess Romix (Rowena), the daughter of King Hengist of Friesland, pressed the beaker with her lippens, and saluted . . . with a Kusjen (little kiss)."

One-Track Mouth

Tell me who first did kisses suggest?
It was a mouth all glowing and blest;
It kissed and it thought of nothing beside.

—Heinrich Heine, *Book of Songs*

Scratch 'n' Sniff

It is highly likely that kissing began as a manifestation of the natural scent attraction between the sexes.

In medieval times, it was believed that a man's well-worn clothing contained aphrodisiacal powers and, if presented to a lady as a gift, was a sure way of winning her love. Such an approach probably wouldn't go over too well today, but the basic idea is sound. A hormonal chemical called pheromone is secreted via male sweat glands, which females (whether they're aware of it or not) find attractive. Women, too, release a sex attractant. In fact, it has been said that Henry III of France fell in love with Marie of Cleves merely by taking a whiff of a sweat-stained garment she'd discarded at a party.

These attractants may well account for the fact that nose rubbing and mutual sniffing of faces, hands, and genitals have been more common throughout man's history than the kiss proper. This is paralleled in the animal kingdom. Prior to intercourse, dogs smell, lick, and bite one another, sea lions rub necks, and elephants put their trunks into each other's mouths. Even moths release a powerful chemical attractant which has, in fact, been bottled in popular perfumes for human use.

Though colognes are said to mask the body's own natural odors, women have, throughout time, used artificial scents for the purpose of *intensifying* their personal aromas. Hottentots applied bachu leaves and butter fat to their bodies, and in Biblical times, women applied wild thyme to their thighs. Italians and Greeks perfumed their lips, and Somalian ladies anointed their private parts with a mixture of burned snail shells, acacia wood, barn stone, and Red Sea sediment. Cleopatra had perfume sprayed on the sails of her boat and, for good measure, between her toes.

In the eighteenth century, a British law permitted a woman using perfumes to be charged with witchcraft. Fortunately, the scent of a woman—whether applied or ingrained—has charmed such archaic statutes into oblivion. Just take a whiff the next time a pretty girl passes by.

Suck on This One

Alfred William Lawson, economist/novelist/physicist of the early twentieth century, believed that kissing and, indeed, all of life, is governed by two basic forces: *suction* and *pressure*. To prove his point, he cited everything from sexual attraction and excretion to the mechanics of the universe and the grasshopper burp. Though kissing fits neatly into Lawson's view of the world, he was nonetheless highly opinionated about the practice: it spread disease and should be *completely avoided*.

3. A Kiss Is Just a Kiss—or Is It?

> The Lover's Kiss, the Mother's Kiss,
> The Little Kiss that says Goodbye.
> The Lonely Kiss upon the mirror,
> The long wet Kiss so slow to dry.
>
> —Anonymous

The Three Kisses of Ancient Rome

1. *Osculum*—for friendship, given on the cheek
2. *Basium*—for affection, given on the lips
3. *Sauvium*—for love, given between the lips

Come Again?

Kisses are forced, unwilling, cold, comfortless, frigid, and frozen, chaste, timid, rosy, balmy, humid, dewy, trembling, soft, gentle, tender, tempting, fragrant, sacred, hallowed, divine, soothing, joyful, affectionate, delicious, rapturous, deep-drawn, impressive, quick, and nervous, warm, burning, impassioned, inebriating, ardent, flaming, and akin to fire, ravishing, lingering, long. One also hears of parting, tear-dewed, savoury, loathsome, poisonous, treacherous, false, rude, stolen, and great fat, noisy kisses.

—Anonymous, quoted in Henry T. Finck, *Romantic Love and Personal Beauty*

Behind Closed Doors

To kiss in private? An unauthorized kiss.
—William Shakespeare, *Othello*

The Lady's Choice

"Stay," he said, his right arm around her waist and her face expectantly turned to him, "shall it be the kiss pathetic, sympathetic, graphic, paragraphic, Oriental, intellectual, paroxysmal, quick and dismal, slow and unctuous, long and tedious, devotional, or what?"

She said perhaps that would be the better way.
—Charles Carroll Bombaugh, *The Literature of Kissing*

Eight Is Enough

Old Magazine reports that eight different kinds of kisses are mentioned in the Scriptures: the kiss of salutation (I Samuel 20:41), the kiss of valediction (Ruth 1:9), the kiss of reconciliation (II Samuel 14:33), the kiss of subjection (Psalms 2:12), the kiss of approbation (Proverbs 7:13), the kiss of adoration (I Kings 19:18), the kiss of treachery (Matthew 26:49), and the kiss of affection (Genesis 27:27). The source adds, "There are some other kinds of kisses which the Scriptures do *not* mention, [and] neither do the young ladies."

The Mother's Kiss:

1. To Son . . .

The purest kiss in the world is this:
The kiss that a mother lays
On her boy's fresh lips
As he blithely trips
To meet the world and its ways.

—Anonymous

2. . . . and Daughter

It was as if I were witnessing the farewell scene when the loving mother once more embraces the daughter and says: "Go out in the world, my child, for I have done all I can for you. Now, take this kiss as a seal on your lips, a seal guarding the sanctuary, to be broken by none unless permitted by yourself. But when the right one comes you shall easily know him." Then she imprints the motherly kiss on the girl's lips, not a human kiss, taking something, but a divine one, giving everything.

—Johannes Jorgensen, *The Diary of the Seducer*

Take Your Pick

Are Germans kiss-crazy? German dictionaries contain no fewer than thirty words for *kissing*, each word denoting a kiss for a different occasion or for a different kind of partner. Here are a few of them: *Abschiedskuss*, good-bye kiss; *Dankkuss*, thank-you kiss; *Liebeskuss* or *Minnekuss*, love kiss; *Morgenkuss*, morning kiss; *Vermählungskuss*, wedding kiss; *Brautkuss*, bride's kiss; *Mutterkuss*, mother's kiss; *Mädchenkuss*, young girl's kiss; *Bruderkuss*, brother's kiss, and so on.

Play It Again

Could Rubinstein himself express a wider range of emotions, by subtle variations of pianistic touch, than our lips can express degrees and varieties of affection in the family, friendly, conjugal, and love kisses?
—Henry T. Finck, *Romantic Love and Personal Beauty*

Beware

Faithful are the wounds of a friend; but the kisses of an enemy are deceitful.
—Proverbs 27:6

A Ruler Might Help

In his 1875 phrenological and physiological study of love, Prof. O. S. Fowler claimed that the lips are the "facial pole" of love, a fact which he said governed the exact locale of a kiss by way of its intent. "Love always kisses its object . . . with the middle of the lips," he explained, "while Friendship and Platonic Love kiss about half way between the corners of the mouth and middle of the lips, and Parental Love with one corner of the mouth."

Armed to the Teeth

There is the kiss of welcome and of parting; the long, lingering, loving, present one; the stolen, or the mutual one; the kiss of love, of joy, and of sorrow; the seal of promise, and the receipt of fulfillment. Is it strange, therefore, that a woman is invincible, whose armory consists of kisses, smiles, sighs and tears?

—Anonymous

Vive La Différence

"William, that was *not* a preacher's kiss!"
—Susan Hayward to William Lundigan in
I'd Climb the Highest Mountain (Fox, 1950)

Meeting of the
Atlantic and Pacific
"The Kiss of the
Oceans"

Canal Statistics.

Length . . . . 40 miles
Channel . . { width at top . . . 500 to 1000 ft.
            { " bottom . 300 to 650 ft.
Time of passage { Through Canal . . 10 hours
                { " Locks . . 3 hours
Gatun Dam { Length of crest . . . . 8000 ft.
          { Extreme width . . . . 2600 ft.
          { Height above normal lake level 90 ft.
Locks { At Gatun . . . . 3 double sets | Average lift 32 ft
      { " Pedro Miguel 1 double set | Length . . 1000 ft
      { " Miraflores . . 2 double sets | Width . . 110 ft.
Culebra Cut . . Length . . . . 9 miles
Total number of men employed 40,000
Estimated total cost, ... $ 375,000,000
Area of Canal Zone . . . . 448 Sq. Miles

Terms of Endearment: Ten Things to Kiss
—and What It Means If You Do

1. *Kiss the bottle / Kiss the cup*—to drink alcohol
2. *Kiss the counter*—to submit to chastisement
3. *Kiss the dust*—to be overthrown or defeated
4. *Kiss the ground*—to be humiliated, to die
5. *Kiss the gunner's daughter*—to be tied to a ship's cannon and caned
6. *Kiss the hare's foot*—to be late
7. *Kiss the post*—to be locked out due to late arrival
8. *Kiss the rod*—to be punished
9. *Kiss the scavenger's daughter*—to be tortured
10. *Kiss the shilling (penny kisser)*—to be cheap or stingy

Eight Things Named After Kisses

1. *Kiss Me Quick.* The name of a popular perfume used by women in 1858.
2. *Kissing Barbie.* "She's the doll who kisses and leaves her mark!" When Mattel Toys' popular Barbie doll turned twenty in 1979, a "kissing" version of the toy was produced. "Press her back," Mattel urged Barbie's fans, "and she tilts her head. See her pucker her lips. Hear the kissing sound! When she wears special lipstick, she leaves a kissing mark!" Barbie, who is scaled after a hypothetical model 5-foot 7-inch in height with a stunning 36-19-35 figure, continued to kiss until 1981. That year, Mattel decided to give Barbie's lips a rest in favor of animating her arms, so that she could apply her own makeup—which must have been sorely needed after so much kissing.
3. *Jump-up-and-Kiss-Me.* The name of a flower in nineteenth century England. It was also referred to as the Look-up-and-Kiss-Me, the Kiss-Me-Ere-I-Rise, and the Kiss-Me-at-the-Garden-Gate.
4. *Kiss-Me-If-You-Can.* A ladies' bonnet sold in America and England in 1850. The name referred to the hat's wide front brim. Another style of bonnet had no brim at all and thus was called the *Kiss-Me-Quick.*
5. *Hershey's Kisses.* Popular mouth-size chocolate drops sold in silver foil wrappings.
6. *Kiss Me, My Darling.* The name of a color that existed in France, circa 1800.
7. *Kissy Suzuki.* A Japanese motorcycle that allows the riders to neck

while driving? Sorry. We stuck this one in to throw you off. Kissy Suzuki is a character in a movie—a Japanese secret agent who "marries" James Bond in *You Only Live Twice* (United Artists, 1967). She was played by actress Mie Hama . . . and certainly lived up to her name.

8. *Angels' Kiss*. A pousse-café consisting of white crème de cacao, crème yvette, Five-Star brandy, and sweet cream.

CHAPTER TWO

How Do I Kiss Thee?

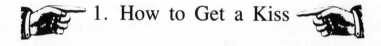

1. How to Get a Kiss

Give me one little kiss . . .
—Molière (Jean Baptiste Pouquelin)
Don Juan

Just Play Dumb

That's how a young fellow who worked as a page in the French court managed to snatch a royal kiss.

There used to be a custom that required pages first to kiss the object they were delivering to a distinguished person. In the process of handing a letter to the princess of Naples, one clever page kissed *the Princess* instead of the letter before giving it to her. He later explained that he'd misunderstood that particular rule of etiquette.

She Wants It

Ask a kiss—and with dissembling
She indifferently grants it.
Ask for none—with secret trembling
Of her heart she really wants it.

And with eyes by sad tears laden,
Silently she is declaring:
Kisses, kisses loves the maiden,
Though she acts as if not caring.

       —Johan Ludvig Runeberg

Follow the Button

One way to get a kiss is to comply with an invitation. For instance, there are buttons you can wear on your lapel that read "Kiss Me!" But does anyone really take them seriously? A nineteen-year-old Iranian fellow did, probably for the last time.

Returning to his Abadan bazaar home in June 1978 after three years of schooling in London, the student noticed such a button being worn by an eighteen-year-old girl who was out shopping with her mother. So, the fellow later explained, "I kissed her." He was consequently put under arrest and jailed for up to three months.

It just goes to show, you can't always believe what you read.

Bridging the Lips

Men who are traveling through the intersection of 52nd Street and Second Avenue in New York City have the ideal opportunity to get a kiss from their female traveling companion. It is, after all, the exact location of one of the original Kissing Bridges, a covered wooden span that once stretched across De Voor's mill stream over a century ago.

Whether traveling by foot, horse, train, or buggy, it was customary for a fellow to request a "toll" of one kiss from the lady nearest him as they passed through the darkened bridge. The term "kissing bridge" came to refer to any one of the 10,000-plus nineteenth-century American covered bridges that provided a couple this romantic opportunity.

Kissing bridges may well have been the inspiration for the Tunnel of Love, the romantic boat ride featured at so many amusement parks. Some tunnels have even sported "Kiss me now!" signs to help motivate the couple into breaking the ice.

The Old Standby

The classic method of getting a kiss is to arrange for you and your intended "victim" to wind up standing together under a sprig of mistletoe. Unless you happen to be in the vicinity of a place where the plant grows wild—eastern and southeastern United States—your best bet will be to wait for Christmas.

The tradition of kissing under the Kissing Bunch, as it is sometimes known, dates back to an ancient Scandinavian myth wherein an evil spirit, Loki, the god of strife, desired to destroy the much-loved god of sunshine, gentle Baldur. Baldur's mother, Frigg, had exacted a vow from all living things not to harm her son, but she forgot the mistletoe. Loki, knowing this, made a dart of mistletoe wood and caused Baldur to be slain with it. After his death, the plant was dedicated in mourning to Frigg, on the condition that it never made contact with the earth, Loki's terrain. Hence it grows on trees, especially appletrees, as a parasite.

In Frigg's possession, the mistletoe was seen only as a symbol of love, and to stress that view, all who passed under it would kiss.

The Druids, and eventually other societies, began to use the mistletoe as a sacred ceremonial entity, used to watch over both priestly kisses and divine human sacrifices. It was believed to cure a variety of diseases, ward off evil, and bring good luck. Greek and Roman warriors dropped their weapons and embraced if it was seen growing on the battlefield. Young girls would sleep with it under their pillows in order to dream of their future husbands.

The tradition of kissing beneath the mistletoe also relates to the ninth century B.C. custom that honored Mylitta, the Babylonian-Assyrian goddess of beauty, love, and fertility. Every woman of that period—in praise of the goddess—was required, at some time of her life, to stand below the sacred mistletoe that adorned Mylitta's temple and willingly give of her body, on the spot, to the first man who approached her.

Today, of course, the lady will settle for just a kiss, thank you.

Watch Out Where You Point That Thing!

If a woman wants a man to kiss her, touching a paper fan to her lips is considered a subtle invitation.

Try This Line

See the mountains kiss high Heaven
And the waves clasp one another;
No sister flower would be forgiven
If it disdained its brother;

And the sunlight clasps the earth
And the moonbeams kiss the sea:
What are all these kissings worth
If thou kiss not me?

—Percy Bysshe Shelley

Ask and Ye Shall Receive

How does one go about getting a kiss from the Pope? Ask Vittoria Ianni. She got one.

The daughter of an Italian street cleaner, Vittoria became the first woman of ordinary station to be kissed by the Pope in a marriage ceremony. John Paul II broke Church tradition in 1979 by marrying Vittoria and burglar-alarm technician Mario Maltese. The Pope customarily marries only those of royal standing, but Vittoria asked, and John Paul obliged.

Taking up Arms

Is there a war under way? And if so, did you participate in it somehow?

If you can answer yes to both these questions, then you should be allowed to kiss any woman you desire without fear of being turned away, regardless of your "ugliness or age." At least, that's how Plato saw it in *Laws*.

Montaigne, however, took strong exception to that philosophy, and spelled out his objections in Chapter 5, Book III, of his *Essays*. It was *his* feeling that Plato's rule not be limited to the military but instead be allowed to extend to "other work."

If She'll Believe This . . .

Kisses kept are wasted;
Love is to be tasted.
There are some you love, I know;
Be not loath to tell them so.
Lips go dry and eyes grow wet
Waiting to be warmly met,
Keep them not in waiting yet;
Kisses kept are wasted.

—Edmund Vance Cooke, "Kisses Kept Are Wasted"

The Executive Approach

At the End of Her Thread

You may have noticed that gloves are no longer in fashion among women. It could be that the ladies got smart and decided to cut their losses.

A custom that originated in colonial New England was that a man who succeeded in taking possession of a lady's gloves was allowed to charge a kiss as the price for their return.

Women who paid up, however, were liable to be prosecuted and fined. Such was the case of Sarah Tuttle, a resident of Connecticut who, in 1660, went next door to borrow some thread. Her neighbor, Jacob Murline, grabbed her gloves and exercised his right. "Whereupon," the New Haven court record later established, "they sat down together, his arm being about her and her arm upon his shoulder or about his neck; and he kissed her, and she kissed him, or they kissed one another, continuing in this posture for about half an hour."

Sarah's belligerent father sued Murline, but Sarah's testimony was purely in the interest of the defendant. Consequently, the judge let Murline off with only a warning. Sarah, on the other hand, was *fined* by the court for having made "excessive payment" on a pair of gloves.

The moral: never run out of thread. Or else *do* run out. Depending.

Heine's Logic

If a girl you want to kiss happens to be holding a large, razor-sharp sword in her hands, it may well be the ideal time to kiss her.

The poet Heinrich Heine thought so, and he was right. A sheriff's daughter, Sefchen, was one day showing off to Heine her late grandfather's mighty sword, while she sang, "Will you kiss the naked sword, which the Lord has given us?" Heine quickly responded, "I will not kiss the naked sword, I will kiss the red-haired Sefchen." Gambling that she'd not resist "for fear of hurting me with the fatal steel," he embraced and kissed her.

Of course, not all women think alike, do they?

Go for It

There's a little Saxon Proverb
That goes very much like this,
That a man is half in Heaven
When he wants a woman's kiss—
But there's danger in delaying,
For the sweetness may forsake it,
So I ask you, tasteful lover,
If you wish one why not take it.

—Anonymous

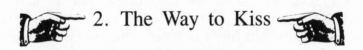 2. The Way to Kiss

The hole in the face is called the mouth
For getting in and giving out,

For every kiss there is a bite,
The tongue hangs long, the lips lock tight.

—Anonymous

Above All Else

"Where do the noses go?"
—An inexperienced Ingrid Bergman to
Gary Cooper in *For Whom the Bell Tolls* (Paramount, 1943)

Know Your Spice Before the Rice

The husband has indeed married too soon if he does not know how kisses
may vary between those who love each other—or cannot make use of this
knowledge, in practice.

—Dr. Theo. Van de Velde, quoted
in *Kama-Chumbana* by R. J. Mehta

Well-Tuned Instrument

Tab Hunter to Gwen Verdon as the seductive Lola: "My teacher said I
have a natural lip. Playing the clarinet, that is."

—*Damn Yankees* (Warner Brothers, 1958)

On the Lookout for Local Lips

Let us drink to the thought that where'er a man roves
He is sure to find something blissful and dear,
And that when he is far from the lips that he loves,
He can always make love to the lips that are near.

—Tom Moore

Czech This One Out

In Prague, Czechoslovakia, the children of Communist officials are
enrolled in dance classes in which "hand-kissing drills" are a regular
feature.

What Does She Have Them for If Not to Grab Onto?

1. Take me by the earlaps and match my little lips to your little lips.
—Plautus, *Asinaria*

2. A lover should not hold his bride by the ears in kissing her, as appears to have been customary at Scotch weddings of the last century.
—Henry T. Finck, *Romantic Love and Personal Beauty*

He Learned It in the Streets

A woman who once kissed Bob Hope asked him, "How did you ever learn to kiss like that?"

"It comes natural, I guess," replied Hope. "I blow up all my own motorcycle tires."

Think About It

A lisping lass is good to kiss.
—John Ray, *English Proverbs*

Just Dessert

Apple pie without some cheese
Is like a Kiss without a squeeze.
—Marie Callendar, Sentiment printed on restaurant napkins

Discipline

Take heed that when upon her lips you seize,
You press them not too hard lest it displease.
—Ovid, *Ars Amatoria*

Kiss 'n' Klop

Advice columnist Dear Abby offered this advice for a gal who complained that her boyfriend's kisses leave her lips raw, bruised, and bloody: "Give him a good klop on the back."

A Gentle Kiss

I'll taste as lightly as the bee,
That doth but touch his flower, and flies away.

—Ben Jonson, "The Kiss"

A Rule of Lip

If you are ever in doubt as to whether or not you should kiss a pretty girl, always give her the benefit of the doubt.

—Thomas Carlyle

Playing It Cool

In *The Art of Kissing*, a 1936 guide to successful osculation, author Hugh Morris advises that the best way to kiss a girl is to corner her against the arm of a sofa. First, flatter her (even if you have to lie), then grab hold,

from *Kiki*, 1931

and finally move in for the kiss. He warns that if the girl reacts by scratching and shrieking out, one should make for the nearest door. "Such girls are not to be trifled with," he concludes.

The Tango Theory

It's better when you help.
—Lauren Bacall to Humphrey Bogart
To Have and Have Not (Warner Brothers, 1950)

Keep Dusting!

Clemens of Alexandria advised all married couples not to kiss within view of their servants.

Low Profile

If you must practise the art of kissing, do it on the quiet and do not tempt others.
—"Rules for Kissing", Kansas Public Health Service

People Are Funny

I twist your arm,
You twist my leg,
I make you cry,
You make me beg,
I dry your eyes,
You wipe my nose,
And that's the way
The kissing goes.
—William Wood, "A Deux"

Watch Your Punctuation

Some lovers are given to romping. A trial of strength punctuated with kisses may end disastrously to the set of his shirt front, and may spell ruin for her frock. These traces are not always to be removed at a moment's notice and may lead to enquiries when the lover has gone. It is better to make the romp general, not particular, if superfluous vital energy has to be worked off in this way.

—G. R. M. Devereux, *The Lover's Guide*

The Old Girdle Trick

Divine Rhodanthe, being prevented from kissing me, held her maiden girdle [a belt or sash] stretched out between us and kept kissing it, while I, like a gardener, diverted the stream of love to another point, lapping up the kiss, and so returned it from a distance, pressing with my lips on the girdle. Even this a little eased my pain, for the sweet girdle was like a ferry plying from lip to lip.

—Agathias Scholasticus

The Height Report

Hugh Morris in *The Art of Kissing* recommends that the man be taller than the woman he kisses, otherwise "the kiss becomes only a ludicrous banality." He adds that "nothing can be more disappointing" than a kiss that is not enhanced by the appearance of male superiority.

Postkiss Suggestion

After you have surrendered yourself body and soul to your husband's kisses, in God's name get to your own bed and lie there quietly.

—Fazil Bey, *Zenan-Nameh*

Ignorance Is Bliss

"I love him because he doesn't know how to kiss—the jerk!"

—Barbara Stanwyck talking about
Gary Cooper in *Ball of Fire* (Fox, 1935)

The Image of Male Superiority Enhances a Kiss (1936 Kissing guide)

The Bottom Line

Now may each and every man
Kiss as best he will and can;
Only I and my sweet miss
Know the proper way to kiss.

—Paul Fleming

3. Where Do I Kiss Thee?

> . . . She kissed his brow, his cheek, his chin,
> And where she ends she doth anew begin.
> —William Shakespeare, *Venus and Adonis*

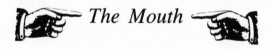 ## *The Mouth*

Many Happy Returns

If kiss you must, do kiss the mouth,
As else you will the joy be missing;
For neither neck nor breast does pout—
The mouth alone returns the kissing.
>   —Friedrich von Logau

Attention All Buds

The taste of the kiss will depend on the mouth of the woman.
>   —Prof. Christopher Nyrop, Ph.D.
>   *The Kiss and Its History*

A Royal Comparison

Just as a rose that opens its calyx when it drinks the sweet dew, she
offered me her sugar-sweet red mouth.
>   —King Wenceslaus of Bohemia

Above and Beyond

Most clearly I remember . . . the feeling of that soft spot just northeast
of the corner of your mouth against my lips.
>   —Lorena Hickok's Excerpt from December 1933 letter
>   to First Lady Eleanor Roosevelt

The Adamance of Lawrence

I have kissed dozens of girls—on the cheek—never on the mouth—I could not.

—D. H. Lawrence
Excerpt from a letter written at age twenty-three

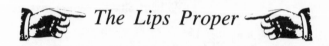 *The Lips Proper*

Naturally . . .

The lips, naturally, are the first erogenous zone.

—James S. Van Teslaar, *Sex and the Senses*

Book Me Up

A soft lip
Would tempt you to eternity of kissing.

—Ben Jonson, *Volpone*

The Most Kissable Lips in the World . . .

. . . are allegedly those of Lois Maxwell, the British actress best known for her portrayal of Miss Moneypenny, M's secretary in the James Bond movies.

In an interview conducted by Mark Greenberg for *Bondage* magazine, Maxwell explained that author Ian Fleming approached her after viewing initial footage from *Dr. No* and said, "When I wrote the part of Miss Moneypenny, I had, in my mind's eye, a tall, elegant woman with the most kissable lips in the world. And you are precisely that."

Now, if only 007 would take notice . . .

Full of Heart

She does wear her heart on her lips, not in the form of words, but more cordially in the form of a kiss.

—Soren Kierkegaard, *Either/Or: A Fragment of Life*

A Gardener's Delight

As if he pluck'd up kisses by the roots;
That grew upon my lips.

—William Shakespeare, *Othello*

Raison d'Être

Teach not thy lips such scorn; for they were made
For kissing, lady, not for such contempt.

—William Shakespeare, *Richard III*

Limited Options

North American porcupines "kiss"—that is, during courtship, male and
female nuzzle one another on their quillfree noses.

Watch Your Lips

The lips are of all the features the most susceptible of action, and the most
direct index of the feelings.

—Sir Charles Bell

Lips Serviced

How many lips have been worn out with kissing at the street door, or in
the entry. . . ?

—Thomas Dekker, *The Seven Deadly Sins of London*

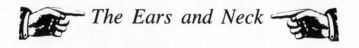 *The Ears and Neck*

The Dangers of Stargazing

She was looking at the stars, and he kissed her neck in the curve beneath
her little chin.

—Paul Williams, *The Knights of Selsby*

Now *That's* Necking—Conrad Nagel and Greta Garbo in *The Mysterious Lady*, 1928

Lord Love an Ear

Ear ye! Ear ye! An eighteenth-century governor of New York, Edward Hyde, Lord Cornbury, kissed his bride, Katherine, on the ears rather than on the mouth when they got married. It was love of Katherine's ears that had originally inspired the marriage proposal. Cornbury devoted entire speeches to those ears, and even urged other men to feel them. So notes Henry Moscow's *Book of New York Firsts.*

Eureka!

One day, indeed, he had kissed not her cheek, but her neck a little below her ear; and Gwendolen, taken by surprise, had started up with a marked agitation which made him rise too and say, "I beg your pardon—did I annoy you?" "Oh, it was nothing," said Gwendolen, rather afraid of herself, "only I cannot bear—to be kissed under my ear."

—George Eliot, *Daniel Deronda*

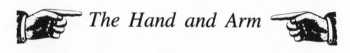 *The Hand and Arm*

The Hand Bone's Connected to the Cheek Bone

What shadow of a right [had he] to go and kiss her hand? He could not pretend to think she had put it out to be kissed. . . .

Mae West and W. C. Fields in *My Little Chicadee*, 1940

She felt there must be something of this kind legibly branded on her face: "Oh! oh! just look at this young lady! She has been letting a young gentleman kiss the palm of her hand, and the feel has not gone off yet; Gyou may see that by her cheeks."

—Charles Reade, *Very Hard Cash*

Got a Minute?

Give me your hand and let me, by a thousand kisses, express the rapture I am in.

—Molière, *Don Juan*

Humphrey's Secret

"But you have not kissed the littlest finger of all. See, it is quite stiff with indignation." . . .

"Marian,—"

"I wonder how many other women's fingers you have kissed—like that. Ah, don't tell me, Humphrey! . . ."

—James Branch Cabell

That's Why He's a Colonel

When serving in Washington, D.C., Lieutenant de Tessan, aide to Marshal Joffre and Colonel Fabry, was approached by a pretty girl who said: "And did you kill a German soldier?"

"Yes."

"With what hand did you do it?"

"With this right hand."

The pretty American girl seized his right hand and kissed it. At this Colonel Fabry said: "Heavens, man, why didn't you tell her that you bit him to death?"

—Edwin Fuller, *Literary Anecdotes*

Ah, to Be Sure!

Only one thing I remember, when she raised her bright lips to me, like a child, for me to kiss, such a smile of sweet temptation met me through her flowing hair, that I almost forgot my manners, giving her no time to breathe.

"That will do," said Lorna gently, but violently blushing; "for the present that will do, John. And now remember one thing, dear. All the kindness is to be on my side; and you are to be very distant, as behoves to a young maiden; except when I invite you. But you may kiss my hand, John; oh, yes, you may kiss my hand, you know. Ah to be sure! I had forgotten; how very stupid of me!"

—R. D. Blackmore, *Lorna Doone*

The Gourmet's Corner

When author Henry James first met novelist Edith Wharton, he kissed her hand. She quickly admonished him: "My dear sir, the flavor starts at the elbow."

Had James visited the Marquesas Islands in their early days, he'd have known better. Marquesan natives, in early times cannibals, considered the female forearm a delicacy.

"The flavor starts at the elbow." © Tomi Ungerer.

Promises, Promises

"Cross my heart, and kiss my elbow."
—Audrey Hepburn in
Breakfast at Tiffany's (Paramount, 1961)

Hands Down

Kissing your hands may make you feel very good, but a diamond bracelet lasts forever.
—Anita Loos, "Broadway Philosophy"

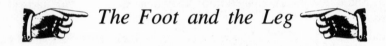 *The Foot and the Leg*

And This Little Piggy

I go down on my knees before you and I kiss your dear feet a countless number of times . . . I long to kiss every toe on your foot and you will see I shall achieve my purpose.
—Fëdor Dostoevski
Excerpt from a letter to his wife, Anna Snitkina

Grateful Were the Women

The English Church once adopted into its marriage rituals an old custom that required the bride, after she was given the ring, to drop to her husband's feet and kiss his right foot.

Down, Boy

Anthea bade me tie her shoe;
I did; and kist the instep too;
And would have kist unto her knee
Had not her blush rebuked me.
—Robert Herrick, "Upon the Nipples of Julia's Breast"

On the Other Foot

According to ancient Hindu custom, a woman was allowed to kiss the feet of a man who was sleeping next to her. However, for a man to do so to a woman was considered quite improper.

A Picture Worth a Thousand Kisses

Famed sculptor Auguste Rodin—whose 1896 sculpture, *The Kiss*, is among his best-known works—laid his reputation on the line when he allowed a stream of kisses to interfere with the stroke of his pencil, according to *The Intimate Sex Lives of Famous People* by the Wallace family.

Having requested and received permission to make a sketch of Ruth St. Denis, Rodin became so overcome by the beauty of the famous dancer's legs that he dropped his pad and began kissing them. The infuriated St. Denis said it proved that Rodin was little more than "an ordinary French sensualist."

Gam-Bit

Fain would I kiss my Julia's dainty leg,
Which is as white and hairless as an egg.

—Robert Herrick

 *Hair*

Her Mane Man

Kissing her hair I sat against her feet,
. Wove and unwove it, wound and found it sweet,
Made fast therewith her hands, drew down her eyes,
Deep as deep flowers and dreamy like dim skies;
With her own tresses bound and found her fair,
Kissing her hair.

—Algernon Swinburne, *Rondel*

Let It Shine

Men: If you're interested in being voted the Most Kissable Head in America, get rid of that hairdo. The judges are all members of an organization called the Bald-Headed Men of America, and to them "kissable" equals "hairless."

Be Gentle

Kiss only soft, I charge you, and beware,
With your hard bristles not to brush the fair.
—Ovid, *Ars Amatoria*

Cut Taxes, Not Beards

The effect of hair on kissing has long been a topic of discussion among scientist and poet alike.

In the Middle East, it was at one time customary for women and children to kiss the beards of their husbands and fathers. Men of the same social class, when greeting, would grab hold of one another's beards and kiss them.

"The chin may be a sexually significant marker for maleness," noted anthropology professor Gordon Hewes of Boulder, Colorado. "Lower face hair surmounting or surrounding the mouth may have both a tactile and visual impact. Some women report that kissing a male with a beard or mustache is more exciting than kissing a clean-shaven mouth."

This view is shared by the women of Holland, who have been quoted as saying, "A kiss without beard is an egg without salt." Ladies in Denmark put it a little more crudely: "To kiss a fellow without a beard is the same as kissing a dirty road."

Perhaps that was the sentiment of many Russian women when, in 1705, Peter the Great proposed a tax on beards. It was an attempt to draw Russians into the mainstream of European life, but it nearly provoked an uprising.

Human Hanky

It is delightful to kiss the eyelashes of the beloved, is it not? But never so delightful as when fresh tears are on them.

—Anonymous

Something to Frown At

It has been said that the females of the Central American Apinaye tribe do much more than kiss their mate's eyebrows during loveplay. Specifically, they bite the man's hair off his brow and spit it out to the side.

. . . *and Beyond*

Decisions, Decisions

Kisses, which, wanton as he strays,
He darts a thousand wanton ways
At mouth, or neck, at eyes, or cheeks;
Him humbly she full oft bespeaks. . . .
—Johannes Secundus, *Epithalamium*

Medieval India's Seven Ideal Places to Kiss

As noted in Kalyana Malla's *Ananga Ranga*, these are as follows:

1. The lower lip.
2. Both eyes.
3. Both cheeks.
4. The head.
5. The mouth.
6. Both breasts.
7. The shoulders.

Downhill Racer

And when the mouth no more the kiss is feeling,
Because the lips' hot fire is creating,
Turn to the cooling Alpine drifts of whiteness.
The arm, its marble splendor not concealing,
May tempt, but not as the soul-penetrating
Kiss pressed upon the bosom's icy brightness.
—Carl Ludvig Emil Aarestrup

Down in the Valley

Graze on my lips, and if those hills be dry,
Stray lower, where the pleasant fountains lie.
—William Shakespeare, *Venus and Adonis*

Smoochathon!

Anatomy of a Kiss

 ## 1. How Long Is a Kiss?

A kiss's strength . . .
Must be reckoned by its length.

—Lord Byron, *Don Juan*

The Sixteen-Day Kiss

It's the longest pair of kisses on record. In a national kissing contest held in May 1983, two couples—Dino De Lorean and Barbara Kane in New York City, and Brad Spacy and Patricia Haugan in Las Vegas—each maintained a kiss for 384 continuous hours. The Vegas pair even threw in twenty-one additional hours for good measure.

Several previous Smoochathons and Kiss-Offs have been held in Florida and Pennsylvania.

Yield to the Lip

A winning kiss she gave,
A long one, with a free and yielding lip.

—William Browne, *Britannia's Pastorals*

But, Officer, We Were Just Getting Warmed Up

A little-known law on the books in Iowa puts a five-minute limit on all kisses that occur within the state.

Reap the Wild Kiss

Stopwatch in hand, legendary movie director Cecil B. Demille clocked a kiss between actress Paulette Goddard and Hollywood fast-food proprietor H. B. Clifford to ensure that it not exceed forty-five seconds in length.

The date was September 19, 1941, and the carefully monitored kiss was a reward which Goddard had earlier offered to any man bringing her the most pieces of aluminum in support of the American war effort. Clifford was declared winner with 365.

Goddard promised that the prize kiss would be "as good" as the one she gave to Ray Milland in the motion picture, *Reap the Wild Wind*. Under DeMille's direction, that kiss lasted forty-five seconds on screen. The copycat kiss, again under C.B.'s guidance, could be no more, no less.

Clifford collected his winning, which he later described as "terrific." He even picked up a few stray smacks on the side.

The Out-of-Towner

Oh, a kiss
Long as my exile,
Sweet as my revenge.
—William Shakespeare, *Coriolanus*

They Never Come up for Air

A kiss can reportedly last for up to twenty-five minutes—if the couple so engaged are "kissing gourami." Gourami are tropical fish, the "kissing" species being a pink or green-white variety that is well known for its habit of kissing its own kind on the mouth.

Long, Wet Kissers

The longest underwater kiss lasted two minutes, eighteen seconds,

Kissing Gourami

according to *The Guinness Book of World Records*. Yukiko Nagata and Toshiaki Shirai performed the 1980 feat in Tokyo, Japan. It was broadcast to curious viewers over Fuji TV.

As Long as a Soul

O love, O fire! once he drew
With one long kiss my whole soul thro'
My lips, as sunlight drinketh dew.
—Alfred Lord Tennyson, *Fatima*

Ten Days on a Dummy

Five members of an ambulance squad spent 240 continuous hours "kissing" a rubber dummy in Clifton, North Yorkshire, England, in 1981. The "kiss of life" (mouth-to-mouth resuscitation) was performed on the inflatable body for a week and a half in order to qualify a team from Clifton's St. John's Ambulance Brigade for a listing in *Guinness*. The total number of individual inflations came to 224,029.

It is not known if the dummy survived.

A Score's Score

Perhaps the longest kiss on record is that which Siegfried gives Brünnhilde in the drama of *Siegfried*. But this is not an ordinary kiss, for the hero has to wake with it the Valkyrie from the twenty years' sleep into which old Wotan had plunged her for disobeying his orders. Thanks to Wagner's art, the thrill of this Love-kiss, magically transmuted into tones, is felt by a thousand spectators simultaneously with the lover.

—Henry T. Finck
Romantic Love and Personal Beauty

As Times Goes By

"Now I have kissed you through two centuries."

—Laurence Olivier to Vivien Leigh, as time takes them from the eighteenth to the nineteenth century in *That Hamilton Woman* (United Artists, 1941)

Long Enough to Go Get Some Popcorn

The longest on-screen kiss in the history of feature films took place between Jane Wyman and Regis Toomey in the 1941 comedy, *You're in the Army Now*. The famous cinema smooch lasted for 3 minutes, 5 seconds—equal to 4 percent of the movie's length.

The Kiss Holds Out

Though in this rapid transit age
To shorten all things is the rage;
Though novel, sermon, poem and play
Grow briefer with each hurrying day,
One bulwark still defies endeavor—
A kiss is just as long as ever.

—Life

2. The Sound of a Kiss

A kiss should be sonorous. Its sound, light and prolonged, takes its rise between the tongue and the moist edge of the palate. It is produced by a movement of the tongue in the mouth and a displacement of the saliva provoked by suction.

—Sheikh Nefzawi, *The Perfumed Garden*

Oh, Those Danes

He kissed her so that the smacking sounded as when you strike the horns off from a hornless cow.

—Danish saying

Reverberation

The sound of a kiss is not so loud as that of a cannon, but its echo lasts a great deal longer.

—Oliver Wendell Holmes
"The Professor at the Breakfast Table"

Ooh, Dat Schmatz!

There are three kinds of kisses based on the sounds that they produce, according to a 1791 study conducted by Austrian scientist W. von Kempelen. The first kind is "a friendly and clear-ringing kiss." The second kind is a more discreet and acoustically weaker version of the first. And the third is labeled an *ekelhafter Schmatz*, translated into English as "a nauseating smack."

Quiet, Please

Loud kisses . . . might betray the lovers to profane ears, and bring on a fatal attack of coyness on the girl's part.

—Henry T. Finck
Romantic Love and Personal Beauty

Religious Experience

He took the bride about the neck
And kiss'd her lips with such a clamorous smack
That at the parting all the church did echo.
—William Shakespeare, *The Taming of the Shrew*

Making Music

[A kiss is] the fiery accompaniment of the keyboard of the teeth of the lovely songs which love sings in the heart.
—Paul Verlaine

Kiss Can't Go Stereo in Philly

A legal battle over whose "kiss" would be heard by all of Philadelphia ensued between two FM radio stations in 1983 and was ultimately settled out of court. WUSL had sought to become WPKS ("Philadelphia's KISS"), but instead backed down to WKSZ, known to listeners as KISS 100. That town just wasn't big enough for the two of them. . . .

Before the Invention of Bug Spray

As if in one single spell, and through the whole evening, was heard a sound similar to the one when someone goes around with a fly smasher—and that was the kissing of those lovers.
—Johannes Jorgensen, *Diary of the Seducer*

Speed Ain't Everything

H. Wendt reports that Roman snails exchange "smacking kisses" while mating.

A Mooving Thought

Mark Twain was fond of quoting a German saying that a kiss "sounds just like when a cow lifts her hind leg out of a swamp."

Surf's Up

The plash of the waves against the pebbles of the beach is like the sound of long kisses.

—Johannes Jorgensen, *Stemninger*

Who Needs Tentacles When You've Got Lips?

"You can imagine how a twelve-foot kiss sounds," pondered film editor Harry Marker back in 1948, referring to the length of celluloid that amounts to a twenty-second screen kiss.

Journalist Patricia Clary took a wild guess: "Like maybe an octopus crawling into a rain barrel?"

A Formula for Eternal Kissing

[Kiss] until it sounds like pulling the horns from an owl.

—Anonymous

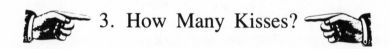 # 3. How Many Kisses?

With a single kiss no woman is caught.

—Romanian proverb

Enough Is Enough

You ask how many kissings of you, Lesbia, are enough for me, and more than enough? As many as the grains of sand in the Libyan deserts, or as the stars that look down, in the silent watches of the night, on the stolen loves of men. If your Catullus, your mad Catullus, could kiss you with as many kisses as that, then perhaps this might be enough.

—Catullus, *Songs*

Enough to Smother the Words

The sentence she was about to utter was lost in a kiss, followed by very many more, the number of which could not be reckoned, and the accurate enumeration of which I shall not attempt because it would certainly be rather long. . . .

—Théophile Gautier

It All Adds Up

"Now," said Edgar, "I kiss you three times on one cheek, and four times on your mouth. How many did that make altogether?"

"Seven," whispered the girl, disengaging herself to breathe more freely.

"That is arithmetic," said the youth, triumphantly.

"Dear me," said Pleasance, "I should not have thought it."

—Lady Wood, *Below the Salt*

Hold the Crème

"Seven sweet kisses and a lump of sugar" used to be the payment offered to men by country women who needed some extra handiwork done.

In Love and War

The only things you may deal out without counting in this life of ours, which is but a little fight and a little love, is blows to your enemy and kisses to a woman.

—Joseph Conrad

The Most-Kissed War Hero

No figure of a popular hero in American public life probably was ever as much kissed as Richard Pearson Hobson, who had distinguished himself in the Spanish American War.

It all began at a big function in Chicago, when two pretty young cousins stood on tip-toe and kissed him. This started the ball rolling, and all the young ladies present, enamoured of the brave young Lieutenant, lined up to kiss him too. Count was kept up to one hundred and then given up. The audience stood by and rooted, calling out, "Good for number 76!" and other helpful comments. The kissing went on for 36 minutes with an average of five a minute. The publicity arising from this incident led to its repetition in every city to which the hero toured. He collected some 10,000 or more in all. A caramel was even put on the market, called "Hobson's Kisses."

—Edwin Fuller, *Literary Anecdotes*

If You Have to Ask . . .

That lady wants me to kiss her. I did it once; isn't that enough?
—Christopher Morley

Blazing Kisses!

At a 1977 speaking engagement in Chicago, filmmaker Mel Brooks was asked by a member of the audience—Wesley—if he would ever consider making a sequel to his movie, *Blazing Saddles*. Brooks said no and explained why:

"It's like kissing the same girl twice. You know how it is, Wesley . . . you kiss her once, that's a breakthrough. Twice, what are you trying to prove?"

"But I *like* doing it twice," said Wesley.

"Then marry the girl, Wesley! Marry her!" urged Brooks. "This time, it's for real!"

The Secret

Pretty red lips as soft as a rose—
How many have kissed them God only knows.
—Anonymous

Odds Are Good for a Guy to Get Kissed

The average female in the United States kisses seventy-nine men before she gets married, according to Dr. Joyce Brothers. Nothing said about *after* she's married . . .

The Bribe

"Wait till we are married, and then I shall kiss you as much as you wish."
—Charlotte to Don Juan in Moliére's *Don Juan*

The Challenge

Allow me nine kisses. Give me eight of them and let me fight for the ninth.

—Dorat

Hold on Nine

A state law in Massachusetts decrees that ten kisses is tantamount to a marriage proposal.

'Tis better to be kissed and caught/than never to be kissed at all.

The Long and the Short of It

Ten kisses short as one, one long as twenty.
—William Shakespeare, *Venus and Adonis*

Nothing Ventured . . .

I ventured a kiss upon her mouth; she resisted a little, but at my entreaty she gave me one in return, and then I took a thousand.
—Nicolas Edme Restif de la Bretonne, *Sara*

Starting Over

Give me a kiss, and to that kiss add a score;
Then to that twenty add a hundred more;
A thousand to that hundred; so kiss on,
To make that thousand up a million,
Treble that million, and when that is done,
Let's kiss afresh, as though we'd just begun.
—Robert Herrick, "Give Me a Kiss"

One for Each New Month

The traditional New Year's kiss was never more appreciated, and perhaps never better utilized, than by a former governor of Nieuw Amsterdam. Each New Year's Day, he would invite local married couples to his home for a celebration, at which time he made a point of kissing all the women present. Even his head usher took advantage of the opportunity to embrace "all the young vrouws." Women with "rosy lips" were particularly sought out, for they were judged to be deserving of "a dozen hearty smacks" from both the governor and his manservant.

Singing the Blues

Here's to the girl with eyes of brown,
If you ask for a kiss she will call you down;
Here's to the girl with eyes of blue,
If you ask for one—she will say, yes, take two.
—Anonymous

The Allowance

Taking his hand now, she led him
Up to the window, and there
Blushing, she willingly let him
Give her a kiss—or a pair.
> —Carl Plong, "A Kiss"

The Third Is a Charm

Your first kiss brought me near to the grave,
Your second kiss came my life to save;
But if a third kiss you'll bestow,
Not even death can bring me woe.
> —Greek folk song

Run for Your Kisses

An exercise study conducted in 1982 by U.C. San Diego's director of human performance, Jim White, determined that people who jog regularly tend to kiss more often than those who don't jog.

Why the difference? I think it's called mouth-to-mouth resuscitation.

Lhasa Lotta Kisses!

In his book *The Origin of the Kiss*, Surgeon Rear-Admiral C. M. Beadnell reports that a devout Buddhist will kiss the ground over 30,000 times while traveling the final six miles along the road leading to Lhasa.

Do *Not* Return to Sender

In three hours I shall see you again. Till then, a thousand kisses, mio dolce amor! but give me none back, for they set my blood on fire.
> —Napoleon Bonaparte
> Excerpt from a letter to Josephine

X Marks the Kiss

The use of an *X* to signify a kiss has been traced to two possible origins:

its employment as a signature by the illiterate, and as a written "blessing" derived from the Christian cross.

Historians have long noted with anecdotal glee the number of such kisses used by famous personalities in their letters. Charles Dickens once printed as many as thirty-nine individual X's in a single correspondence. Lewis Carroll, who penned about two thousand letters a year, wrote to Gertrude Chataway that she sent him so many kisses in a letter that he had to pay for excess postage.

In a letter to his wife, Mozart offered 2,999½ kisses. Fortunately, he didn't mark each one a separate X. Too many of those, advises Foulsham's *Complete Letter Writer*, is "vulgar."

Barrymore Got the Most

The most kisses in any one movie were the 191 parceled out by John Barrymore in Warner Brothers' 1926 production of *Don Juan*. That's about one kiss per minute.

It is said that 66 percent of those kisses went to two women in particular: co-stars Mary Astor and Estelle Taylor. All things being fair, that gave each lady 63½ kisses.

Now you know why agents and lawyers come into play.

20,009 on Nine—and Let Her Ride

David Ward of Manchester, England, bestowed 4,079 kisses on just as many girls during a single eight-hour stretch in 1983. Paul Trevillion pulled off 20,009 kisses during a mere two-hour period in Cleveland eight years earlier . . . but he had 4,078 fewer women to juggle. Sadie Nine was the single recipient of each of Paul's smacks. The latter two reportedly supplemented their rigorous kissing exercises with a second sport: cycling.

Pain Killer

If you by kissing have made sore
My lips, then kiss me all you please.
Kiss until night, and kiss me more,
For only thus I'll be at ease.

—Anonymous

Take One After Every Missing Kiss

Have you ever felt that you didn't kiss someone *enough*? Don't worry; all is not lost. A *Nachkuss* can easily remedy the situation. The word is a German term used to define a kiss that is given for the express purpose of "making up for kisses that have been omitted, or supplemental kisses."

The Perfect Solution

My wish . . .
That womankind had but one rosy mouth,
To kiss them all at once from North to South.
—Lord Byron, *Don Juan*

The Plea

One kiss more—one more.
—Arthur Schnitzler, *Hands Around*

Memorable Kisses

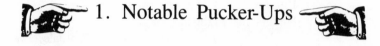 1. Notable Pucker-Ups

To kiss or not to kiss is one of the most important questions of the twentieth century: a question which is normally answered no and acted yes.

—Dr. Albert Ellis, *The Folklore of Sex*

Saved by the Song

"A flower of Deborah's choosing!" The cry was taken up, and the young girl rose and stepped up to Othman er-Riffa.

He looked at her boldly; and then, since he dared not speak to her with his lips, he spoke to her with the flash and depth of his eyes.

"I love your hair!" said his black eyes.

Her brown eyes caught the message and sent back answer, silent, demure, yet heavy with sudden longing:

"Then why don't you kiss me?"

"I love your mouth!" said his black eyes.

"Then why don't you kiss me?" replied her brown eyes.

"I love your throat!"

"Then why don't you kiss me?"

"I shall—presently!" said his black eyes, and he bowed as, blushing, amidst the laughter and cheers of the crowd, she took a crimson rose from her wedding bouquet and gave it to him.

Once more he broke into song, improvising couplets in her honour.

—Achmed Abdullah, *Steel and Jade*

The Look

Strephon kissed me in the spring,
Robin in the fall,
But Colin only looked at me
And never kissed at all.

Strephon's kiss was lost in jest,
Robin's lost in play,
But the kiss in Colin's eyes
Haunts me night and day.

—Sarah Teasdale, *The Look*

Jay-Kissers

That glance of theirs, but for the street, had been a clinging kiss.

—Alfred Lord Tennyson, *Merlin and Vivien*

From the Horse's Mouth

Roy Rogers' horse, Trigger, was able to simulate the action of "throwing kisses" due to his unique talent of "puckering his lips convincingly."

Kiss and *Don't* Make Up

Hollywood makeup man Wally Westmore told *Look* Magazine in 1937 that Mae West, following love scenes in movies, would rarely need any touching up since her kissing style hardly disrupted her makeup. The reason, perhaps, was that most of the sex symbol's kisses occurred in the pucker-ups.

"I never kissed a man in my plays, and seldom on the screen," she confessed in a 1968 interview with the Associated Press. "I always felt that the look before the kiss was more important than the kiss itself. I figured it was better to fade out before the kiss and let the audience use its imagination."

The old adage "less is more" was apparently best for West—leaving less of a mess for Westmore.

Lip-Worthy

Her lips, whose kisses pout to leave their nest,
Bid man be valiant ere he merit such.
                              —Lord Byron, *Childe Harold*

The Ages and Ages of Aquarius

Linda Goodman's Sun Signs (Bantam Books, 1971) warns that Aquarian men may take an unusually long time getting around to a good-night kiss. However, Ms. Goodman hastens to add, "It's well worth waiting for."

Pre-Carnal Knowledge

"Usually by the time I kiss a guy I already know his mother's maiden name."
                              —Goldie Hawn to a gynecologist in
                              Private Benjamin (Warner Brothers, 1980)

Worth the Wait

She wanted him to kiss her, and waited an eternity. And when he had kissed her, and she was in a maze of rapture, a tiny idea shaped itself clearly in her mind for an instant: "This is wrong. But I don't care. He is mine"—and then melted like a cloud in a burning sky.
                              —Arnold Bennett, *The Price of Love*

The Final Effort

The last thing newspaper magnate William Randolph Hearst did before he died on August 14, 1951, was to pucker his lips for a kiss that never came. His extramarital love, Marion Davies, had been at Hearst's side that fateful day. At one point, in the morning, she stepped out of the room. Hearst puckered his lips for a kiss, as he did each evening to kiss

Marion good night, but this time she was not there. Finding no lips to meet his own, Hearst promptly expired.

Never Even Got There

When in the course of conversation, she puts her hand on mine, and carried away by the exchange of words, comes closer to me, so that the heavenly breath of her mouth reaches my lips, then I believe that I must sink to the ground as hit by lightning.

—Johann Wolfgang von Goethe
Die Leiden des Jungen Werthers

Tell and Kiss

Just now the vogue in amorous scenes is for the woman to slip her hand and arm round the hero's neck and draw him nearer to her. . . . Personally if I am told to do a love scene in my own way I put my hands on the man's breast. It seems to me there is a decided suggestion of sex in a woman putting her arm round a man's neck and pulling him closer to her. But if the director insists that you do it that way, the actress of course has to comply.

—Estelle Taylor, *Movie Magazine*, 1924

Irresistible Resistance

Her countenance with the beautiful eyelashes she turns aside when I try to raise it for a kiss: by thus struggling she affords me the same delight as if I had attained what I desire.

—Kalidasa, *Malavika and Agnimitra*

The Freak-out Kiss

The *hanuvatra* was an old Hindu style of *almost* kissing. According to ancient love manuals, the couple would move "the lips toward one another in an irritating way, with freaks, pranks, and frolics." After "some time," however, "the mouth *should* be advanced, whereupon a kiss would finally occur."

They Blindfold Horses, Don't They?

I always carried a number of sterilized blindfolds, which I would casually place over each baby's eyes before I kissed it. This prevented its growth from being stunted through terror.

—W. C. Fields, *Fields for President*

 # 2. The First Kiss

To a woman the first kiss is the end of the beginning; to a man it is the beginning of the end.

—Helen Rowland

God's Kiss of Life

The very first kiss, in a metaphorical sense, was the kiss from God which filled man with the spirit of life, causing him to become a rational soul. This is according to the account of Genesis (2:7), in which God is said to have formed man from dust. This religious concept of divine insufflation frequently uses the kiss metaphor in its depiction.

Heavenly Delight

The angels see in love's first fervent kiss
A true reflection of their own high bliss.

—Johan Ludvig Runeberg

Intoxicating Delight

She threw her arms around Dain's neck and pressed her lips to his in a long and burning kiss. He closed his eyes, surprised and frightened at the storm raised in his breast by the strange and to him hitherto unknown contact, and long after Nina had pushed her canoe into the river he remained motionless, without daring to open his eyes, afraid to lose the sensation of intoxicating delight he had tasted for the first time.

Now he wanted but immortality, he thought, to be the equal of the gods.

—Joseph Conrad, *Almayer's Folly*

Packs a Wallop

The first kiss that the [Muslim] bridegroom gives is equal to 180 years of worship. It also enables him to escape the torments of the tomb, causes a light to be shed over his grave and procures the ministerings of eighty angels.

—Sir Richard Burton

The First of Its Kind

My lips till then had only known
The kiss of mother and of sister,
But somehow, full upon her own
Sweet, rosy, darling mouth—I kissed her.

—E. C. Stedman, *The Door-Step*

The Kiss That Started a Career

Track star Bruce Jenner recalled that, as a teenager, he was terrified over giving a girl a first kiss. When he did finally get up the nerve to do it, he shot a quick peck to his date's cheek and took off as fast as possible in the opposite direction. "That was the beginning of my track career," he noted.

The Peppermint-Drop Effect

He took courage, and surrendered himself to sensations experienced for the first time in his life. The unparalleled and unprecedented had happened. His neck, still feeling the embrace of two soft, scented arms, seemed anointed with oil; near his left moustache, where the kiss had fallen, trembled a slight, delightful chill, as though from peppermint drops; and from head to foot he was stirred with new and extraordinary sensations, which continued to grow and grow.

—Anton Chekhov

The First Movie Kiss. May Irwin and John C. Rice, 1896.

The First Movie Kiss

The first kiss ever recorded on film for commercial entertainment was performed by actors John C. Rice and May Irwin in a thirty-second nickelodeon production. Adapted in 1896 from the famous Rice-Irwin kissing scene in the Broadway comedy, *The Widow Jones*, the couple's kiss was filmed in close-up—another first—by Raff and Gammon for Vitascope. It became an instant hit.

The Kiss, as it came to be known, also drew the wrath of self-proclaimed moralists, who were shocked by it and feared what might follow. One of those was Chicago publisher Herbert Stone, who called the film "absolutely disgusting" and "indecent in its emphasized vulgarity. Such things call for police interference."

First Kiss, Second Lady

He had scarcely closed the door behind us when we shared our first kiss. . . . I shall never, never forget how Mr. Harding kept saying, after each kiss, "God! . . . God, Nan!" in high diminuendo, nor how he pleaded in a tense voice, "Oh, dearie, tell me it isn't hateful to you to have me kiss you!" And as I kissed him back I thought that he surpassed even my gladdest dreams of him.

—Nan Britton's account of an illicit New York rendezvous with Warren G. Harding

The Beginning of the Rest

He who has gain'd a kiss, and gains no more,
Deserves to lose the bliss he got before.
If once she kiss, her meaning is express'd;
There wants but little pushing for the rest. . . .

—Ovid, *Ars Amatoria*

Dark Passage

I'm ruined! I'm ruined!
—Carry Nation
The temperance crusader's reaction to her first kiss,
delivered in a dark hallway in 1865 by
Dr. Charles Gloyd of Ohio, later her first husband

Medicinal Poison

The second kiss will, I am sure,
The evil of the first one cure.

—Dorat

 3. The Kiss-and-Tell

The greatest sin 'twixt heaven and hell
Is first to kiss and then to tell.

—Anonymous

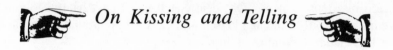 *On Kissing and Telling*

The Origin of the Kiss-and-Tell

An ancient law of Rome stated that any virgin who could prove that she'd been kissed would be awarded full marriage rights.

Who-Dunnit

"From now on, I've got to know the *name* of every man that kisses me."
—Ida Lupino in *Artists and Models* (Paramount, 1937)

The Curse

Here's to the girl that gets a kiss,
And runs and tells her mother;
May she live and die an old maid,
And never get another!

—Anonymous

Depositers Beware

A sign posted in a bank said: "Don't kiss our girls—They're All Tellers!"

Refrain Thyself

And if he needs must kiss and tell,
I'll kick him headlong into hell.
—Nathaniel Cotton, *Burlesque upon Burlesque*

Try as One May

How much can a kiss be described?
—Lafcadio Hearn

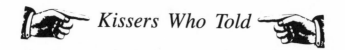 # Kissers Who Told

Vivien Leigh and Cammie Conlon

"Scarlett, kiss me. Kiss me once."

Once was apparently enough. According to *Gone with the Wind* trivia experts, Vivien Leigh complained that costar Clark Gable had bad breath. But that didn't alter the course of the script. Rhett and Scarlett had a child in the movie, portrayed by four-year-old Cammie King. Forty years later, as Cammie Conlon, she recalled a kiss that Gable gave her in the classic film. Nothing about his breath, though. Rather: "His mustache scratched."

Hilda Doolittle

During her engagement to famed poet Ezra Pound, Hilda Doolittle maintained a diary in which she described Pound's kisses with three distinctive words: "fiery," "magnetic," and "electric."

Nonetheless, the engagement did not last.

Thomas Dean Matthews

At the age of eighteen, Thomas Dean Matthews experienced "the biggest moment in my life" when, in May 1974, he got kissed by fugitive heiress Patricia Hearst during a drive-in movie.

On the run from the FBI, Hearst and SLA fugitives Bill and Emily Harris had commandeered Matthews' van, with Matthews inside, and drove to a drive-in theater in Inglewood, California. During the movie, Matthews later recounted, Patty—an alleged kidnap victim herself—"leaned over and kissed me" in the rear of the van.

"It wasn't a long kiss," added Matthews, "but she kissed me on the lips. She was neat . . ."

In a classic case of kiss-and-tell, Matthews' testimony about his experience eventually helped to bring charges of firearms violation and bank robbery against Patty Hearst.

Kay Summersby

His [Dwight Eisenhower's] kisses absolutely unraveled me.

Tony Curtis

After a bit of cinematic osculation in the movie *Some Like It Hot* (United Artists, 1959), Tony Curtis complained that kissing Marilyn Monroe was "like kissing Hitler."

Nicchia Oldoini

The beautiful nineteenth-century Italian secret agent, Nicchia Oldoini, kept a detailed diary, in which her numerous romantic escapades were described in a special code. According to the authors of *Intimate Sex Lives*, the letter *B* referred to a kiss (*bacio* is "kiss" in Italian). The combination of *BX* meant "beyond a kiss." Not satisfied to leave well enough alone, she also employed a final rating: *F*.

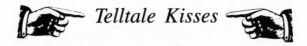 *Telltale Kisses*

From Paris with Love

At a seventeenth-century banquet in Brahan Castle, Scotland, the hostess—wife of Kenneth, third Earl of Seaforth, at the moment far off in Paris—asked the psychic Brahan Seer to look into his magical crystal and "see" what her absent husband was up to. Kenneth, said the Seer, was at that moment kissing the hands of another woman. Infuriated, the countess ordered the Seer dropped, head first, into a heap of hot tar.

Pod'n My Kiss

In Daniel Mainwaring's 1956 screen adaptation of Jack Finney's science fiction novel, *Invasion of the Body Snatchers*, a kiss is used as a device to detect the existence of emotionless alien "pod people" in the bodies of human beings.

Toward the end of the movie, Dr. Miles Bennell (Kevin McCarthy) leaves his sleepy ladylove, Becky Driscoll (Dana Wynter), alone in a cave while he scouts the terrain. When he returns, he finds her asleep (a definite no-no, since sleep is the state that allows "body snatchers" to do their thing). Miles shakes her awake and, in a romantic moment, kisses her. Becky's reaction—or rather, *non*reaction—to the kiss, reveals to Miles in no uncertain terms that all that is left of his woman is her shell.

Art Imitates Life—Sometimes

Gilbert Stuart, the early American portrait painter, once met a lady on the street in Boston who saluted him with, "Ah! Mr. Stuart, I have just seen your miniature, and kissed it, because it was so much like you."

"And did it kiss you in return?"

"Of course not!" she answered, laughing.

"Then," said Stuart, "it was not like me."

—Edwin Fuller, *Literary Anecdotes*

An Original

Painter Jo Baer had not intended to include the image of a pair of lips in her original composition, but it was nonetheless added by an art lover in 1977.

When a passerby came across Baer's $18,000 work in an Oxford, England, museum, she thought it looked "cold." So—she kissed it "to cheer it up." Unfortunately, the red lipstick stains it left required $1,260 of restoration work, and the well-intentioned museum visitor ended up in court.

The Scene of the Kiss

Although the kiss has never gained "official" public acceptance in Japan, it *has* become very popular among the country's police officials. A new method of crime detection—*lip printing*—was invented in 1971 by Doctors Kazuo Suzuki and Yasuo Tsuchihashi of the Tokyo Dental College. Like fingerprints, no two "lip prints" are alike. By having suspects kiss a piece of glass, police can compare prints with those found on glasses, cigarettes, napkins, and the like at the scene of a crime.

Given this development, a suspected criminal can refuse to talk, but his lips may nevertheless betray him.

Deception

Why dost within thine arms me lap
And with false kisses me entrap?

—Anonymous

The Kiss of Betrayal

A kiss was used to betray Jesus Christ by one of his disciples in the year 29 A.D., according to the New Testament (Matthew 26:48–50, Mark

Giotto's *Kiss of Judas*

14:44–46). Judas Iscariot was paid thirty pieces of silver by Jewish leaders to identify Jesus in the Garden of Gethsemane, which he did by kissing him. "Judas," said Jesus, "betrayest thou the Son of Man with a kiss?" (Luke 23:48) Jesus was subsequently arrested and executed.

Reading into a Kiss

One of the many escape plans devised to break abolitionist John Brown out of jail in 1859 involved the kiss of a beautiful young woman.

Details of the proposed rescue were to be written on a small piece of paper and passed surreptitiously to the prisoner, mouth-to-mouth, by way of an amorous kiss from a female visitor. Brown, however, refused to take part in any escape, correctly believing that the abolitionist cause would be better served by his martyrdom.

The Down Payment

A woman who permits a man to kiss her will ultimately grant him complete possession.

—Dr. Iwan Bloch
Sexual Life in England, Past and Present

Look up Before You Kiss

A kiss given beneath a mistletoe was considered tantamount to a marriage proposal by the ancient English.

Wife Tasting in Old Rome

In the interest of safeguarding the purity of women, the republic of ancient Rome maintained a law that forbade females to drink wine. Another law, *jus osculi*, permitted the kissing of women by all close relatives and was often used by suspicious husbands for the purpose of enforcing the liquor law. In other words, kisses were frequently utilized by men to see if their wives had been hitting the bottle on the sly.

Licensed to Kiss

Cinema's James Bond 007—or "Mr. Kiss-Kiss, Bang-Bang," as the Italians call him—was saved by a very revealing kiss in his third film adventure, *Goldfinger* (United Artists, 1964).

After blowing up a heroin refinery in Latin America, Bond (Sean Connery) pays a social visit to a sultry young woman, Bonita—who is, of course, right in the middle of taking a bath. Bonita steps out of the bath water and embraces Bond for a sensuous kiss. In the midst of this kiss, Bond sees the reflection of an approaching thug in Bonita's pupil. As the attacker prepares to strike, Bond spins 180 degrees with Bonita still firmly in his grasp, allowing the lady to take the blow. Needless to say, 007 kills the menacing intruder for disrupting what *had* promised to be a most enjoyable evening.

It's just a lucky thing spies don't close their eyes when they kiss!

The Kiss That Threatened a Government

An 1835 attempt to overthrow a government in India hinged on a kiss between a conspiring minister, Jota Ram, and his mistress, Rupa.

After poisoning the government's ruler, Jota and Rupa ordered one of their agents, Narana, to drop the rightful heir, a baby, from a thirty-foot-high royal terrace to its death on the courtyard floor below. The signal for Narana to proceed with the staged "accident" was a kiss, to be passed from Jota to Rupa at the far end of the yard.

The kiss indeed triggered a murder—but not the prince's. It seems the plot had already been uncovered by a servant and the royal baby switched with a commoner, who died in his master's place. The baby prince lived to rule, the conspirators were jailed for life, and the government remained secure.

 4. Kisses Stolen and Forced

A stolen kiss is only half a kiss.
—Henry T. Finck, *Romantic Love and Personal Beauty*

Martial's Preference

I do not care for kisses, unless I have snatched them in spite of resistance.
—Martial, *Epigrams*

A Biting Decision

According to an eighteenth century traveler through the American backwoods, biting off a woman's nose was a standard penalty for adultery in certain American Indian tribes. It was also prescribed by some Hindu religious authorities, sometimes in conjunction with removing the wife's hair and lips, throwing her to the dogs, and parading her naked through the city on a mule.

A reversal of this nose-biting punishment was once established in England for use as recourse against stolen kisses. As a matter of fact, that law is reportedly still on the books there.

The celebrated case that set the precedent for this ruling was Newton v. Saverland, 1837. Thomas Saverland had made a pass at Caroline Newton in an effort to swipe a kiss. Resisting, Newton literally took a bite out of Saverland's nose. The injured party took the woman to court, but the presiding judge ruled in Newton's favor. "When a man kisses a woman against her will," he declared, "she is fully entitled to bite his nose if she so pleases." "And eat it up!" added Newton's lawyer.

A Royal Promise

Do thou snatch treasures from my lips,
And I'll take kingdoms back from thine!
—Richard Brinsley Sheridan, *The Duenna*

High Risk Kiss

Linda K. Pennoyer filed a $100,000 suit against insurance man Raymond C. Largent over a kiss and its aftermath that took place in Oregon in 1973. Ms. Pennoyer charged that Largent kissed her in his office "against her will," and when she "withdrew" from him, she fell down and hit her head. Hopefully Largent had covered himself.

Don't Be Foolish

By forgiving him at first sight, you foolish girl, you deprived yourself of many pleasures,—of his prostration at your feet, of a kiss passionately stolen.

—*Seven Hundred Maxims of Hâla*
third century A.D. Indian writer

But If 1 Percent Be Willing . . .

There is no pleasure, except in a man slightly perverted, in kissing a girl entirely against her will.

—Clement Wood, "The Art of Kissing"

What's a Woman to Do?

The issue of women's rights as they relate to forced kissing was addressed in great detail by a German jurist toward the end of the eighteenth century. His opinion on the matter was formally set down in a treatise he wrote that divided up every kind of kiss into two categories: *permissible* and *unpermissible*. The former section contained sixteen entries, the latter only two.

For the most part, the jurist based his findings on two factors: *social standing* and *intent*. For instance, "a lady of nobility" who is forcibly kissed by a commoner wields tremendous punitive power, while a servant girl kissed by that same man has virtually no redress. Also, said the juror, it is the woman's burden to prove a lustful intent in the kiss, since German law at that time defined all kisses as "chaste" unless proved otherwise.

Regarding the use of defensive measures against the kisser, the jurist said that "a box on the ear" was acceptable—*unless* it was inflicted with an "Amazon fist."

Furthermore, any woman who provoked a kiss with a line such as "I'd like to see the one who dares kiss me" would have no case whatsoever.

The Pacifier

In medieval India, forced kissing was considered permissible between husband and wife in certain circumstances. Called the *milita* kiss, it was given by a man to his wife if she was angry or in such a bad mood that she would not willingly kiss her husband. The man was to "forcibly fix his lips upon hers and keep both mouths united till her ill-temper passes away." There was, of course, no provision for *his* ill temper.

Needing the Eggs

Kissing an unwilling pair ov lips iz az mean a viktory as robbin' a bird's nest.

—Josh Billings, "Kissing"

Steal Away

The eighteenth century Danish author Ludvig Holberg once noted that in Naples, he who stole a kiss from a woman in public was ordered, by rule of law, never again to set foot within a thirty-mile radius of that city.

It's All in the Muscles

There once was a maiden of Siam,
Who said to her lover, young Kiam,
  "If you kiss me, of course
  You will have to use force,
But God knows you're stronger than I am."

                         —Anonymous

The German Opinion

A forcible kiss is like a corn on the foot.

Naughty Is Nicer

You will find, my dear boy, that the dearly prized kiss,
Which with rapture you snatched from the half-willing miss,
Is sweeter by far than the legalized kisses,
You give the same girl when you've made her a mrs.

—Anonymous

The Immorality of It

In June 1977, a Johannesburg, South Africa, court fined twenty-six-year-old Chrisostome Magubane $230 for kissing a woman on the cheek in an elevator. Amour Loren had accused Magubane of leaning against her, kissing her cheek, and saying, "You are married to me."

Judge I. J. J. Luther found the defendant guilty, not because he stole a kiss, but because he was black, and she was white, and thus his action violated the 1950 Immorality Act that forbids interracial sex.

"My dignity was injured because he was a stranger to me and black," Loren testified, adding that the resultant shock caused her to get out of the lift on the wrong floor.

Shocking, indeed.

The Preface

Do not make me kiss, and you will not make me sin.
—H. G. Bohn, *Hand-Book of Proverbs*

In the Know

"I saw you take his kiss!" " 'Tis true."
"Oh, modesty!" " 'Twas strictly kept:
He thought I slept; at least, I knew
He thought I thought he thought I slept."
—Coventry Patmore, *The Angel in the House*

Easy Come, Easy Go

The kiss that's stolen now is kissed
And gone for good; however,

The kiss that's kissed is seldom missed
So much as the kiss that's never.

—Puck

 # 5. Yes, We Have No Kisses

Ah, years may come and years may go,
But ne'er shall I forget
The sweetest kiss I'll ever know—
The kiss I did not get.

—Anonymous

Better Late Than Never

There is no Japanese word for "kiss." That is because kissing has never
been an accepted Japanese custom, either romantically or socially. In
fact, in 1926, the kiss was officially proclaimed "unclean, immodest,
indecorous, ungraceful and likely to spread disease." Even Rodin's
famous sculpture, *The Kiss*, was secreted behind a bamboo curtain while
"on display" with other European artwork during a Far East tour. And
American movies certainly didn't remain intact for Japanese audiences; in
a single year, up to 800,000 feet of cinematic osculation would wind up
on the floor instead of the screen.

But things *may* be changing. A recent survey taken for the prime
minister's office by the Japan Society for Sex Education showed that 33
percent of the males and 26 percent of the females between the ages of
sixteen and twenty-one practice kissing regularly. That bamboo curtain
may slide away yet.

Taking No for an Answer

H: I love you to distraction! You are the only woman that ever made me
think she loved me, and that feeling was so new to me, and so delicious,

Rodin's *The Kiss*

that it "will never from my heart." Thou wert to me a little tender flower, blooming in the wilderness of my life; and though thou shouldst turn out a weed, I'll not fling thee from me, while I can help it. Wert thou all that I dread to think—wert thou a wretched wanderer in the street, covered with rags, disease, and infamy, I'd clasp thee to my bosom, and live and die with thee, my love. Kiss me, thou little sorceress!

    S: Never.

H: Then I'll go: but remember I cannot live without you. . . .
—William Hazlitt, recounting an exchange between himself and
Sarah Walker, in his book *Liber Amoris or the New Pygmalion*

Really Stuck-Up

An old book devoted to social manners in Baghad—*Kitâb almowaschâ*—
reports that it was the custom of Oriental women to entice a man by
withholding kisses and, in their place, sending him a piece of gum that
she had already chewed.

The Exclusivity Rule

I tried two years in vain, while courting my wife, to get her to kiss me;
but she would not, and I married her because she wouldn't. I wouldn't
marry any girl who would. The more she wouldn't, the more I wanted to
marry her; for I wanted kisses from one whose kisses were exclusive.
—The "ablest criminal lawyer in Illinois," 1875

Stop the Wedding!

As late as the 1930s, engaged Laplanders did not kiss one another. The
couple was to appear modest, and the bride-to-be was expected to protest
the marriage the night before the ceremony.

Just Hop off the Buss, Gus

In ancient India, one of the ways for a woman to rid herself of an
unwanted husband or lover was "Not giving him her mouth to kiss." If
that failed, twenty-six other possibilities remained. (Paul Simon, take
note.)

Oscar's Regret

Actress Grace Kelly, one of the Oscar presenters at the 1956 Academy
Awards, was harshly criticized days later by columnist Louella Parsons
for failing to offer a kiss during a key moment of the Oscar ceremonies.

M.C. Jerry Lewis had just paid a warm on-stage tribute to the princess-to-be, yet Miss Kelly did not acknowledge it in any way.

"It seems she might have taken a moment to thank him," wrote Parsons, "to give him a little kiss or something before leaving the stage so abruptly."

She'll Sleep Through Anything

It was a prince's kiss that possessed the magical properties needed to awaken a beautiful princess from her enchanted sleep in the classic fairy tale, "Sleeping Beauty." In tracing the story to its origin, however, it becomes apparent that key elements of its plot have undergone a metamorphosis through the ages.

The now-famous kiss was first incorporated into the legend in Charles Perrault's 1697 version, "La Belle au Bois Dormant." But two other tales, "Pentamerone" (first printed in France in 1528), and "Perceforest" preceded Perrault's. In these original versions of "Sleeping Beauty" *no* romantic kiss was used to awaken the princess. Instead, the dashing prince finds the sleeping beauty, falls in love with her, rapes her, and leaves.

Dashing, indeed . . .

Beware of Greeks Wearing Beards

In ancient Greece, males generally wore beards. Egyptians, on the other hand, disliked beards. Because of this, it is claimed, "no Egyptian of either sex would on any account kiss the lips of a Greek."

A Kiss for the King

Saudi Arabia's King Faisal, in 1975, was in his office taping a TV discussion with the Kuwaiti oil minister when he had an unexpected visitor. The king's nephew, Prince Faisal Aziz, suddenly and without announcement, pushed past a guard and entered the king's office. King Faisal rose to his feet and bowed his head to the Prince, expecting his nephew to bestow a traditional kiss in honor of Muhammad's birthday. But there was no kiss—only bullets. Gun in hand, the prince fired once into his uncle's head and again into his neck, killing him. Three months later, the prince was publicly beheaded for his crime.

Code of the West

King of the Cowboys Roy Rogers refused to kiss women in his movies—
"*except*," he conceded, "maybe for kissing her on the cheek like a
sister."

The reason for this was to avoid upsetting his young male fans. "We'd
get tons of letters from boys saying, 'Leave out that mushy stuff,'"
explained Rogers. The only problem was that young girls did like some
romance, hence the cheek-kiss compromise.

In general though, Rogers and wife Dale Evans followed a simple
code, which was even enforced by studio management: "Cowboys don't
kiss girls."

Brotherly Love

First-born sons of the Pacific's Hervey Islands are prohibited from ever
kissing their sisters. An Indian writer suggests the reason for this is an
"apprehension of mutual danger," or fear of incest, which is reportedly
common among certain primitive cultures.

Warm the Heart

> The most intimate embrace
> Leaves the heart cold and unsatisfied—
> If the rapture of the kiss is wanting.
>
> —Arabian proverb

Hold Your Tongue!

Most snails don't kiss; they rub antennae. Makes sense, when one
considers that a snail's tongue contains more than 14,000 teeth.

The Way of the Kiss

 1. Carry on Kissing

And if you'll blow to me a kiss,
I'll blow a kiss to you.
—Horace and James Smith, "The Baby's Debut"

Stand up and Be Kissed

It is customary—at most formal social occasions, at least—for gentlemen to stand when a lady enters the room. Six hundred years ago, however, there existed a stringent social code in France that not only brought *women* to their feet when a well-to-do *man* walked in, but saw to it that she kissed him on the mouth, as well. This practice was even carried out in the midst of church services, resulting in frequent disruption among the congregation.

There were, of course, those who objected. "It is contemptible," wrote Montaigne, "that a lady must be obliged to reach her lips to every one who comes with a couple of servants behind him, no matter how repugnant to her he may be; and we of the male persuasion do not gain anything by it, as we have to kiss half a hundred by no means handsome women for every two or three who may be considered pretty."

Blowing in the Wind

I throw a kiss across the sea,
I drink the winds as drinking wine,
And dream they are all blown from thee,
I catch the whispered kiss of thine.

—Anonymous

Kiss on the Hand Worth Two in the Air

The gesture of kissing one's own hand and then "throwing" or "blowing" the kiss into the air originated centuries ago as an expression of adoration toward a god, yet it is used commonly in today's fast-paced society as a "kiss-on-the-run," thrown to a friend or lover across a room or street.

In some cultures, people kissed their hand with no intention of blowing it off. Alpine peasants did this prior to accepting a gift, and children of various nationalities have been taught to kiss their own right hand when given candy. This display of gratitude has persisted through time, but the object of affection has changed. Now the gift or prize itself is occasionally kissed, not the hand that takes it.

Au Contraire

Many kiss the hand they wish cut off.

—George Herbert, "Jacula Prudentum"

Kissy-Kissy

One might assume that social kissing is on the increase, what with all the friendly busses that are exchanged between both friends and strangers at parties and get-togethers. Kisses are frequently seen flying right and left, landing on mouths, cheeks, and most especially pockets of air only scant millimeters away from the face.

These kisses are not new at all and in fact flourished among the upper classes of the sixteenth century.

An excerpt of a letter written on October 29, 1544, from one Annibale Caro to the duke of Parma tells of a particular gathering at the Bruxelles home of Emperor Charles V:

"Kissing among the ladies [was] highly interesting. Not the most prominent of the men alone, but all of them, took each one a lady. The

Spaniards and the Neapolitans were the most anxious. It was a cause of great merriment when the Countess Charlotte de Pisseleu, in the attempt to kiss the emperor, craned her neck from the saddle where she sat till she glided down and kissed the ground instead of the monarch. The emperor hurried to help her up and gave her then a real good kiss, and a generous smile on top of it. Close behind came the Duke Ottavio, riding. He jumped quickly from the horse, and was immediately led by the emperor to the queen sitting in a carriage with other ladies. The duke kissed the queen, and went off, but the emperor called him back, telling him to kiss the other ladies too."

A Period Kiss

Centuries ago, in various parts of the world, a kiss was the key element in village rituals celebrating a young woman's first menstruation. In a town initiation ceremony, the local women would line up and kiss the "lady of honor." Though such a fuss over menstruation might seem ridiculous to modern-day women, the kissing ritual doesn't seem half-bad when compared with the customs and beliefs of certain primitive tribes, who often barred menstruating women from barnyards, vineyards, grainfields, or other areas where her condition could bring "bad luck."

And in This Corner . . .

When women kiss, it always reminds one of prizefighters shaking hands.
—H. L. Mencken

Keeping the Tools in Order

I saw two maiden ladys kiss yesterday on the north side ov Union Square five times in less then ten minitts; they kist every time they bid each other farewell, and then immediately thought ov sumthing else they hadn't sed. I couldn't tell, for the life ov me, what they sed, or what they sed waz the effekt of the kissing. It waz a which-and-t'other scene.

Cross-matched kissing iz undoubtedly the strength ov the game. It is trew thare iz no statu ragulashun against two females kissing each other; but i don't think thare is mutch pardon for it, unless it iz done to keep tools in order; and two men kissing each other iz prima-face evidence ov dead beatery.
—Josh Billings, "Kissing"

A Kiss Qualified

So the Captain of the thieves pressed forward and looking upon the prisoner, knew him, whereupon he went up to him and strained him to his bosom and threw his arms round his neck, and fell to kissing him upon his mouth. (As he would kiss a son. I have never yet seen an Englishman endure these masculine kisses, formerly so common in France and Italy, without showing clearest signs of his disgust. R.F.B.)

—Sir Richard Burton, *Thousand Nights*

Slobberers Unwelcome

In the country, where great lubberly brothers slobber and kiss one another when they meet . . . 'Tis not the fashion here.

—William Congreve (speaking of seventeeth-century England)
Way of the World

Love Thy Neighbor?

Every neighbor, every hairy-faced farmer presses on you with a strongly scented kiss. Here the weaver assails you, there the fuller and the cobbler . . . there one with bleared eyes, and fellows whose mouths are defiled with all manner of abominations.

—Martial (speaking of kisses among men in ancient Rome), *Epigrams*

With Kisses Torn Asunder

Dutch scholar and humanist Desiderius Erasmus traveled to England in 1497 and was so overwhelmed by the abundance of kissing he encountered that he wrote the following letter to his friend, the poet Faustus:

"They have a custom which cannot be too much honoured. Wheresoever you go a-visiting, the girls all kiss you. With kisses you come in, with kisses depart; returning they kiss you again. Cometh one to you, the kisses fly between; doth she go way, with kisses you are torn asunder; meeting in any place, kisses abound. Go where you will, it is all kisses. Indeed, my Faustus, had you but once tasted of lips so fragrant and so soft, on my honour you would not wish to reside here for ten years only, but for life!"

Commencement Kisses

Kisses were a major part of the graduation proceedings for apprentices in seventeeth century Germany.

Each apprentice mechanic about to become a full-fledged journeyman was required to invite a young woman to attend the ceremony as his personal "wreath virgin." As the exercises began, each virgin painted a large mustache on her man's lip, while the senior journeyman placed a crown on his head. The virgin then kissed the fellow and replaced the crown with a wreath. Following a brief speech, the journeyman boxed the youth on the ear three times, qualifying him for yet another kiss from the virgin. She then washed the mustache off his face.

Afterward, everyone attended a reception where the new journeymen were allowed to kiss each girl present at a cost of one mark per kiss.

It is not known why this practice fell out of favor. But should it ever be reinstated, enrollment figures may well skyrocket.

 You May Now Kiss the Bride . . .

Among the Romans, the future Couple sent certain pledges one to another, which, most commonly they themselves afterwards being present, would confirme with a religious Kisse.

—William Vaughan, *The Golden Grove*

A Hitch in Time

All the fuss about kissing the bride is part of civilized man's tendency to ceremonialize key stages or relevant aspects of life. Among some primitive peoples, men raided neighboring tribes and carried off as many brides as they could seize. There was no pact, nor kiss with which to seal the deed. According to legend, the early Romans abducted women from their neighbors, the Sabines, to populate their city-state.

Surprisingly, those days are not over. Today, men of the Kirghiz S.S.R. in the Soviet Union still follow the ways of their nomadic ancestors: they see, and they conquer. There's just one hitch, however. Today the abducted wives can file charges of bride stealing against their paramours. The penalty: three years in jail.

It just ain't like it used to be. . . .

Thumbs Up, and Chug-A-Lug

The original purpose of the nuptial kiss was to bring about a full spiritual union between bride and groom by exchanging the "breath of life." Forerunners to this gesture included the pressing together of moistened thumbs, or drinking—in the presence of friends and family—a mixture of the couple's own blood.

Honeymoon for One

Among the tribes of Morocco, kissing was the means by which a newlywed man symbolically overcame the bashfulness he supposedly felt toward his parents following the marriage ceremony. In some instances, the man would disappear for three weeks, returning to his bride and parents only in the company of his best man and one bachelor. Hoods covering their faces, the three would enact a ritual of kissing the groom's parents' heads. Once done, the shy husband moved back in to join his new wife.

Whipping up a Kiss

The nuptial kiss was performed under duress in the marriage rites of White Russians. The bridal couple would get in bed together, and the best man would beat the groom three times with a whip, demanding, "Look at each other, kiss, and embrace fast!"

The Parson's Privilege

It has been said that the Scots initiated the custom whereby the officiating clergyman kisses the bride. The belief was that the bride's happiness was dependent on this kiss, so, in every ceremony, "the parson . . . claimed it as his inalienable privilege to have a smack at the lips of the bride immediately after the performance of his official duties."

In the original Catholic service, kisses became rather contagious. The groom acted as a sort of middleman, taking a kiss from the priest, and passing it on to his bride. The priest's kiss also went to an assistant, who had the rigorous job of sharing it with the entire wedding party.

Kiss Me Quick!

During medieval times, the wedding kiss was actually an important legal procedure called *osculum interveniens*. Its purpose was to solve the dilemma of what to do with the wedding gifts in the event the bride or groom should die prior to completion of the full marriage ceremony. Without that kiss, an untimely death would necessitate return of all the presents. But once the kiss was exchanged, the presents stayed, no matter *who* keeled over.

Why Eloping Was Invented

German law during the Middle Ages required that a newlywed couple exchange much more than a kiss at the close of the wedding ceremony. A wedding was not considered over until the guests personally ushered the couple into bed. Since law held that the newlyweds may not be legally recognized as joint owners of their collective property until "the coverlet is drawn over their heads," it was necessary that there be witnesses to the marriage's consummation. Hopefully the bedroom was large enough to accommodate everyone.

The Bride's Prerogative

"Kiss me, I'm nervous."
—Goldie Hawn to Burt Reynolds, anticipating wedding plans in *Best Friends* (Warner Brothers, 1982)

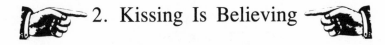 2. Kissing Is Believing

Itchy nose, kiss a fool.
—Proverb

Attention All Butterfingers

You've heard of throwing spilled salt over your left shoulder to avoid bad luck? In Denmark, they're similarly concerned about dropping bread. No, they don't hurl loaves and slices over their shoulders. Instead, bread that is dropped must be kissed. (They don't say whether or not you still have to eat it.)

A Rock Kisser's Delight

The Blarney Stone is a triangular piece of limestone said to possess the power of endowing those who kiss it with fluent and persuasive speech.

Its history dates back to 1446 when Cormac the Strong, chief of the MacCarthy clan, decided to rebuild his old wooden castle in stone. In the process, he caused the family's venerated inaugural stone to be cemented into the structure, thus assuring that it would not be carried off (as the Scots' Stone of Scone had been by the English). From this sturdy fortress, his descendants were able to defy the English, even the powerful Elizabeth I. The sixteenth-century MacCarthy is the one who created the "Blarney" legend. He put the queen off with fair words so often that when one of his flattering speeches was reported to her, she replied, "It's all Blarney; what he says he never means." Since then, any man with a gift for cajolery or glibness has been said to have "kissed the Blarney Stone."

Blarney Castle is currently in ruins (blown up by Cromwell in the seventeenth century), but the magical Blarney Stone remains in the wall of the castle's inner tower, one hundred feet above the ground. The site draws tourists from all over the world, who want to climb the tower just to kiss the famous stone. Those who do must hang from their heels through a castle parapet in order to reach it. In 1932, an Irish boy tried but didn't make it; while trying to plant his kiss, he slipped and tragically fell to his death.

Castle officials, who must wash lipstick stains off the rock every morning, get their jollies by occasionally leading visitors to the *wrong* stone.

Kissing Fast

Saint Agnes was a thirteen-year-old girl said to have been executed during the fourth century for rejecting a state-arranged marriage. Inspired by her legend, a romantic superstition developed among teenagers of England. They believed that by refraining from all kissing on January 21, Saint Agnes' Day, they would be assured of meeting their destined love in the very near future.

Do the Kiss-and-Shuffle

An old French superstition claimed that if one kissed a deck of cards before starting to play, winning was assured. (Wanna bet?)

No Tongue Unturned

Man has about 9,000 taste buds on his tongue. Throughout time, he must have come up with at least as many ways to poeticize the various tastes of a woman's kiss. Consider, for instance, this passage from the *Song of Solomon* (4:10):

> Thy lips, O my spouse, drop as the honeycomb,
> Honey and milk are under thy tongue.

Few poems, however, reveal that which women have found under a *man's* tongue. In medieval times, it was a ball of wax containing the tongue of a sparrow . . . or, as Pennsylvania Dutch women discovered, the raw heart of a dove. It was the belief that if a man kissed the woman he desired with either of these under his tongue, he would be sure to win her.

Such a surprise-filled smooch could have been the reason Tibetans started the practice of sticking out their tongues at one another in lieu of a kiss. (They'd also concurrently hold their right ear and rub their left hip, but that was probably just to make it look good.)

Sealed with a Kiss

> Make them kiss the book.
> —Anonymous
> *The Manner of Keeping a Court Baron*

The custom of kissing or touching a book of law or Scripture while taking an oath or pledge dates back many centuries to the belief that one could guarantee a promise by imbuing it with supernatural power. This was done by citing the name of a divine being in whom one had faith, while concurrently making physical contact with a holy object representative of that deity.

In classic times Romans would place their forefingers on their testicles when giving evidence (hence our words *testimony* and *testament*) or a Bedouin judge would touch a witness' phallus to ensure that truth would be spoken. Holy relics and books were touched in the same way. A kiss was frequently used, however, in the belief that it transferred the essence of one's soul through the breath of the kiss.

Frequently, the oath was a "curse in waiting" against the taker, who was well aware that a supernatural punishment would befall him if he violated the oath or perjured himself. This theory is rooted in tribal contract ceremonies in which oaths were made between individuals while holding weapons between their teeth, indicating that that weapon would be used against the party who reneged on the deal. Of course, it couldn't have been easy reciting an oath with a spear between one's teeth . . . which is probably why they finally stopped doing it.

Even If It's Your Wife?

If the first person you see after waking up in the morning is an old woman, you could be in store for some bad luck. This can be avoided, so say ancient beliefs, by kissing the woman.

The Soldier's Promise

Want to get married and settle down? If you're a woman, one way to start might be to catch the next plane out to northern Italy. Travel to the city of Ravenna and locate the Academy of Fine Arts. Inside you'll find a marble statue of the famed sixteenth-century soldier, Guidarello Guidarelli. Kiss him. On the lips. No, you won't be arrested on the spot. You will, however, be joining about 5 million other women who have done the very same thing.

Though the reclining, armor-clad figure was sculpted by Tullio Lombardo nearly five hundred years ago, a rumor was started in the late 1800s that any woman who kissed the statue would marry and settle down with the man of her dreams. A century of superstitious females have since sought out and kissed Guidarello's marble lips. Not surprisingly, those lips now sport a reddish glow.

They All Kissed the Bride . . . and Then Some

The custom of kissing the bride after the wedding ceremony dates back to old Scotland, when the young wife was required to kiss every male in attendance. (Lest you think those Scots lasses were gullible, it should be

*"Lost in the magic of your kiss, I forgot about
the potato salad. Bring home a quart."*

noted that a collection plate was passed around immediately thereafter.) A
similar English belief held that he who kisses the bride *after* the ceremony
but *before* the groom kisses her will be granted a year of good luck.

A related custom is that of communal bride deflorations, which were
practiced by tribes in East Africa, Peru, Australia, New Guinea, and the
West Indies. In these public ceremonies, the bride spent her wedding
night with each of the male wedding guests in turn (based on seniority).
This was done to protect the husband from the evil that was believed to be
associated with defloration. In fact, priests or kings were sometimes
recruited for this task, since they were supposed to be particularly potent
in overcoming such evil. This is perhaps the source of the droit du
seigneur, the medieval idea that a man's feudal lord had the right to have

first sexual relations with his vassal's bride on her wedding night—a right probably not exercised except in rare cases. On the Canary Islands, a child that was the product of such a mating was *preferred* to one born of the husband. This is because ordinary husbands produced commoners, while royalty created only noble offspring.

And a Bill from the Cleaners

It has been said that a kiss from a chimney sweep will bring good luck.

Light My Fire

Superstitions relating to kissing under the mistletoe abound. One belief was that if a girl did not get kissed under one at Christmas time, she could be assured that she would not be married within the coming year. Then again, even if she *did* get the kiss—according to another belief—neither she nor the one she kissed would *ever* get married if the mistletoe was not destroyed by fire on the twelfth night after Christmas. Sometimes you just can't win. . . .

A Silver Lining

An old German belief prescribed a sure-fire protection against being hit by lighting. One must cross his or her heart, then kiss the earth three times.

Kisses from Heaven

The lore of kissing offers a tidy explanation for the existence of clefts and dimples on a person's body: Those cute indentations are said to be imprints created by the kisses of angels.

Dispelling the Myths

> A kiss won't harm you dear,
> Have no fear;
> It won't make babies
> Nor make your dimples disappear.
> > Recited by a minor player in—
> > *Dinner for Adelle* (Dimension Pictures, 1979)

The Kiss Under the Bridge

"There is an old Venetian legend that lovers who kiss in a gondola under the Bridge of Sighs . . . at sunset . . . as the bells of the Campanile toll . . . will love each other forever."

Those are the words of Julius Edmond Santorin—as spoken by Laurence Olivier—in the movie, *A Little Romance* (Orion Pictures, 1978). Julius is a lovable con artist who befriends Lauren and Daniel, two runaway teenagers with a crush on each other. When Julius tells them that he read of the legend in Elizabeth Barrett Browning's diary, and that it had indeed come true not only for the Brownings but for Julius and his late beloved wife, Lauren and Daniel decide that they, too, must seal their destinies with a legendary kiss.

The kids later become disillusioned, however, when they discover that Julius had fabricated the story. The ashamed but well-meaning old man nonetheless fights to keep their flame of young love alive. "You could *make* it come true," he says. "What are legends, anyway? Mostly stories about ordinary people doing extraordinary things. . . . Something that two people who are in love create together—against impossible odds— can hold them together forever."

Julius, believed by authorities to have kidnapped the kids, is eventually arrested, while Lauren and Daniel race against time to fulfill the legend before sundown. Under fierce interrogation, Julius refuses to reveal the kids' whereabouts until he hears the bell of the Campanile toll. Knowing that all is now well, he admits that the kids are "in a gondola just going under the Bridge of Sighs."

"What for?" he is asked incredulously.

A lump in his throat, Julius replies: "A kiss."

The Kiss That's Worth a Hill of Buns

At early English marriage ceremonies, small, spicy-tasting buns brought by the guests would be stacked up high on a table. The bride and groom then stood on opposite sides of the table and tried to kiss over the hill of buns. A successful kiss meant they would be prosperous and content for life.

How Germs Spread

Sneeze on Tuesday, you kiss a stranger.

—Old superstition

But Does the ADA Approve?

Cancel that dental appointment! A nagging toothache may be instantly relieved by following an ancient German custom: kissing an ass on his muzzle. Just be sure to use the right end.

The Hostage Kiss

The exchange of a kiss to symbolize a pledge of agreement has its history in ancient voodoo rites. Among some native tribes, saliva—like blood, hair, or nail clippings—was seen as an extension of the being and could therefore be used in black magic rituals to bring harm to a person. Consequently, an exchange of saliva was often used to enforce contracts, since each party could hold hostage something of immense value belonging to the other. If the two were in a big hurry, the exchange was made quickly in a kiss or, less eloquently, by spitting into each other's mouths.

Oil's Well That Ends Well

In sixteenth-century Italy, girls would spirit away baptismal oil from their church and apply it to their lips before kissing a man. Their superstition was rooted in the verse they would recite prior to the kiss:

> I take not oil for my affliction,
> But I take the benediction
> From this Saint———
> That it may move the man I love . . .
> [Translation from the Italian by Charles Leland]

A girl named as her patron any male saint whose image was illuminated by an oil lamp.

Hopefully, the mystery of the church's depleted oil reserves ultimately found a solution in the confessional.

Clothes Call

By this time I had kissed Moggy two or three times, and she began to be freer with me; and when I pressed her to marry me the next morning, she laughed, and told me it was not lucky to be married in her old clothes.

—Daniel Defoe, *Colonel Jack*

Kisses Heard Round the World

 1. Scandalous Kisses

Is your mother scandalized because you have given me a kiss? Why, if that's the case, then take it back, my dearest, and make your mother satisfied.

—Anonymous

The Kissgate Scandal

Manilius, a senator of ancient Rome, was censured and officially rebuked for an act he was caught committing in broad daylight. Bribery, perhaps? Kickbacks? Blackmail or political spying? Not at all. The senate was scandalized because of a kiss Manilius was seen giving his wife *in the presence* of their daughter.

This Never Happened to the Other Fella!

A short-lived movie industry scandal surrounding the making of the United Artists movie *On Her Majesty's Secret Service* took place in London in 1969.

George Lazenby, an Australian model, inherited the role of James

Bond from actor Sean Connery by starring in the new Ian Fleming adventure. His costar was Diana Rigg, a seasoned stage actress best known for her TV series, *The Avengers*. After filming a number of love scenes, Lazenby reportedly told an interviewer that his costar had eaten garlic before their kissing sequences in order to "bug" him. Infuriated by such headlines as "Bond Bugged by Bad Breath and "Rigg Eats Garlic Before Kiss," the erstwhile *Avenger* fired off a letter to the editor, denying the garlic charge and labeling the new 007 a "fathead."

Lazenby confirmed that he and Rigg "weren't speaking at the end of the picture," and guessed that "Diana mistook my nervousness as a newcomer for pettiness."

Years later, after leaving the Bond role because of a falling out with the producers, Lazenby recalled that the entire Garlic Affair had actually been manufactured by the British media, a wild exaggeration of a facetious remark that Rigg had made to him in the studio commissary about their being sure to eat garlic before an upcoming kissing scene.

Which is the *real* story? Perhaps the British Secret Service will look into it. . . .

Not With My Wife, You Don't!

During the Middle Ages, a bishop took the liberty of kissing the wife of Rudolf of Hapsburg. In doing so, he created quite an uproar. Rudolf, it turned out, was something of the jealous type. Infuriated over the extramarital kiss, he ordered the bishop banished from Hapsburg, not to return until after Rudolf was dead and buried.

A Spiritual Kiss with Too Much Spirit

Jesus Christ told his disciples (John 14:27), "Peace I leave with you; my peace I give unto you," and Saint Paul urged the masses to "salute one another with an holy kiss" (Romans 16:16) as a symbol of that peace. Adapted by the Church for ceremonial use, this holy kiss of peace became a regular part of early Christian "love feasts." However, it was not long before the practice got out of hand, with promiscuous kisses proliferating among the congregation regardless of one's sex. It gave rise to great scandal until, in 397, the Council of Carthage announced a ban on all religious kisses between men and women.

By the twelfth century, someone in England invented a "kissing machine" to replace the practice of interpersonal kissing. The device was called an *osculatorium* or *pax* and consisted of a handled plaque made of ivory, metal, or wood inscribed with a cross, an image of Christ or the Virgin Mary, or other sacred design. It was kissed first by the priest, then passed around among the congregation.

Unfortunately, aristocracy was soon claiming a "right" to kiss the device before all others during services. In addition, the kiss's spiritual application again gave way to its natural carnal association when young men discovered the romantic novelty of kissing the osculatorium immediately after a pretty girl had touched her lips to it.

So, with scandal again on the rise, the osculatorium fell out of use, and Pope Innocent III forbade *all* kissing during services. By 1312, the Catholic Church had decreed that unmarried couples who kissed were guilty of committing a sin if there was an intent to follow it up with fornication.

Today, a gesture of peace is often made among worshippers, with a handshake, kiss on the cheek, or a kind word.

Navy Wanted Cat off Its *Finback*

A kiss that occurred on a nuclear submarine in July 1975 resulted in the censure of the sub's skipper by the United States Navy.

Commander Connally D. Stevenson, commanding officer of the *Finback*, a hunt-and-kill sub, had allowed visiting go-go dancer Cat Futch to perform topless in front of the sub's crew on the *Finback*'s port fair water plane. Following the dance, which Stevenson's lawyer later described as a "fun thing," the commander escorted Futch onto a pilot boat and gave her a farewell kiss on the cheek. Futch had been aboard the sub for three days, but it was that farewell kiss that drew the ire of his superiors. In a formal letter of reprimand, the Navy criticized the kiss, explaining that it "tended to demean the position" of Commander Stevenson.

The skipper's attorney said that the sub's crew viewed Cat as "an entertainer" who had become a friend of all the men on board.

An Emperor Who Threw Them

Otho, Emperor of Rome in A.D. 69, was much criticized for his public kissing. No—he wasn't taken to task for indiscreet necking. Rather, his habit of throwing kisses to his followers was attacked as "slavish." Otho

The Fingertip Kiss

only held the throne for about three months, so perhaps "slavish" is too mild a way to describe how the Romans felt about this habit.

Use of the "fingertip kiss," as it is known, has often been held in disrepute by guardians of social etiquette. In his 1558 book of manners, *Galateo*, Italian archbishop Giovanni della Casa calls the gesture a "barbarous and strange . . . ridiculous custom; a practice wretched in itself, and still further prostituted by a promiscuous use of it on all occasions. . . ."

Leonore's Choice

Washington, D.C., was thrown into a momentary tizzy in May 1981 over a greeting given by United States chief of protocol Leonore Annenberg to Britain's Prince Charles during his visit to the States.

Some Americans were up in arms over a curtsy that Ms. Annenberg gave the Prince on his arrival here, but White House Deputy Press Secretary Larry Speakes tried to quell the uproar by pointing out that on his departure, the prince got a kiss from Leonore instead. A State Department spokesman explained that various welcome gestures had been given consideration, including "running up and throwing one's arms around him and giving him a big kiss."

The Mummy's Kiss

Scandal ripped through Paris in 1907 because of a long and passionate kiss performed on stage at the Moulin Rouge theater.

Author/actress Colette and her close friend, Missy, the Marquise de Morny, set out to shock their audience at the January 3 premiere of Missy's mime ballet, *Rêve d'Egypte*, in which both women were starring. The play was about an Egyptian mummy who awakens from her eternal sleep, unwraps her bandages, and recalls her ancient love affairs.

In a key scene, the near-nude Colette embraced Missy (who was dressed as a man) and the two exchanged a prolonged, erotic kiss. It literally caused a riot in the audience, which happened to include Missy's ex-husband, the Marquis de Belbeuf, and some distinguished friends.

A French newspaper called the play's kiss "a scene so repugnant that the audience was forced to intervene," resulting in a "revolting scandal."
—The production was quickly retitled and Missy replaced with a male actor. Future audiences, however, continued to believe that there were still two females cavorting and thus heckled the players during the kissing scene. But by the time the curtain came down, the theater echoed with sincere applause.

Now *That's* Patriotism

A kiss exhanged between actors Peter Finch and Murray Head in the 1971 United Artists movie *Sunday, Bloody Sunday* was one of the first times two males kissed one another in a close-up in a major film. The British story of a bisexual love triangle was originally to have shown the controversial embrace from afar, but director John Schlesinger daringly chose to move the camera closer. He later recalled that Finch and Head "were certainly less shocked by the kiss than the technicians on the set." When asked about the kiss by an interviewer, Finch replied jauntily, "I did it for England."

North Meets South—Briefly

A presidential kiss and its aftermath echoed across the land in 1979 when President Carter greeted Jacqueline Bouvier Kennedy Onassis with a kiss on the cheek and got a harsh grimace in return.

The occasion was the dedication of the John Fitzgerald Kennedy Library in Boston, Massachusetts. Carter, a native Georgian, reportedly bussed a number of women in attendance, yet none reacted as JFK's widow did.

A possible reason for Mrs. Onassis' annoyance at the President's Southern hospitality was put forth by former Kennedy adviser Arthur J. Schlesinger Jr. "In the North," he told the *New York Post*, "gentlemen do not kiss ladies on such brief acquaintance." Or perhaps, in the North, it's just a lot colder all around.

 # 2. Five Newsmaking Kisses

We have kissed away Kingdoms and provinces.
William Shakespeare
Antony and Cleopatra

The Kiss That Overthrew a King

Rollo the Ganger, the viking whose invasion of northern France in A.D. 890 resulted in his acquiring the dukedom of Normandy, went to pay his respects to the French king, Charles the Simple. He did not feel like leaning over to kiss the king's foot, as was the custom, so instead he lifted Charles's foot up to his mouth. The laws of balance and gravity being what they are, Charles was tipped backward off his throne. Onlookers were reportedly unable to contain themselves. Charles, on the other hand, had no choice *but* to contain himself. Coming from a powerful viking vassal, lazy kisses must be swallowed along with one's pride.

A Feast for Sore Eyes

As many as three hundred women were in the running for the opportunity to give the Official Kiss to famed scientist and statesman Benjamin Franklin at a feast held in his honor at the French court. "The handsomest of [the] 300" was ultimately selected for the task. The lucky lady laid a laurel wreath on his head and, as the 299 losers looked on, kissed both of Franklin's cheeks.

Detente, Indeed

A soured friendship was repaired by a kiss in Moscow on June 8, 1880. Two of Russia's most famous novelists, Fëdor Dostoevski and Ivan Turgenev, buried their ill will after Turgenev was moved by a speech Dostoevski made at a Pushkin festival. Ivan approached Fëdor and kissed him, exclaiming, "You're a genius, more than a genius!"

The Most Equal Kiss

Brancusi's sculpture *The Kiss*, created of yellow limestone during the early 1940s, was notable for its unique depiction of absolute male/female equality. Unlike other versions of the artist's *Kiss* renderings, this one is totally symmetrical and completely void of elements suggesting either submission or domination. Man and woman are differentiated strictly by hair detail and curvature of the female breast.

Be They Humble

At a 1975 Mass in Rome's Sistine Chapel commemorating the tenth anniversary of a truce between the Vatican and the Eastern Orthodox Church, Pope Paul VI performed a special gesture of humility by kissing the feet of Metropolitan Meliton of Chalcedon, the representative of the Eastern Church. Meliton was surprised by the Pope's action and tried to reciprocate, but the pontiff would not allow it, so Meliton kissed Paul's hand instead. The dramatic event was in marked contrast to the excommunications the two churches had conferred on each other some nine hundred years ago.

3. The Power of the Kiss

For love or lust, for good or ill,
Behold the kiss is potent still.
—John Richard Moreland, "The Kiss"

More Dangerous Than the Scorpion

"What do you think will happen to you through kissing a pretty face? Won't you lose your liberty in a trice and become a slave, begin spending large sums on harmful pleasures, have no time to give to anything fit for a gentleman, be forced to concern yourself with things no madman would care about?"

"Heracles! what alarming power in a kiss!" cried Xenophon.

"What? Does that surprise you?" continued Socrates. "Don't you know that the scorpion, though smaller than a farthing, if it but fasten on the tongue, inflicts excruciating and maddening pain?"

"Yes, to be sure; for the scorpion injects something by its bite."

"And do you think, you foolish fellow, that the fair inject nothing when they kiss, just because you don't see it? Don't you know that this creature called 'fair and young' is more dangerous than the scorpion. . . ?"

—Xenophon, *Memorabilia*

Flapper Zapper

"She just glues herself to a man and drains the strength out of him."
Anonymous Hollywood description of actress
Theda Bara's method of kissing

The Kisses That Shortened a Prison Term

In "The Night of A Thousand Eyes" episode of *The Wild Wild West* TV series (CBS, 1965), a beautiful but deadly assassin, Jennifer Wingate (Diane McBain), is transported to a federal prison by secret service agents

James West (Robert Conrad) and Artemus Gordon (Ross Martin) aboard their private train.

While discussing the prison term awaiting her, Jennifer embraces Jim (whom she'd previously tried to kill) and gives him a passionate kiss.

"Life," insists Jim after the kiss, reiterating the prison sentence.

Another passionate kiss, as Artemus looks on. "Five," says Jim, amending the sentence.

Yet another kiss. "And of course," he adds, "time off for good behavior."

Artemus' jaw has dropped in disbelief. "Jim!" he exclaims incredulously. "How can you sit there and let yourself be stung by the kiss of death?" Jennifer turns to Artemus and gives *him* a long kiss. "On the other hand," mumbles Artie, recovering, "there's no reason to be vindictive, either. . . ."

Deadlier Than Dynamite

There ought to be no doubt as to the dangerousness of a kiss; the peril is indeed greater than the one connected with dynamite or gun cotton. For, as a matter of fact, people don't go fooling around with such explosives in their pockets, whereas they always have a kiss at hand, or shall I say at the mouth. And then, when the dynamite has exploded you are rid of it, but there is no such thing as exhausting the supply of kisses without getting it replenished in the very attempt to exhaust it. For the kiss you give you reclaim in the act of giving, and the one you receive you instantly redeliver, neither party sustaining any loss.

—Prof. Christopher Nyrop, Ph.D., *The Kiss and Its History*

The Kisses that Melted Metal

The lips of worshipping masses have worn away, over the years, great pieces of metal. The mouth and beard of the bronze statue of Heracles in Agrigentum in Sicily was kissed so many times that it virtually vanished. Another bronze statue, that of Saint Peter in Rome, has lost most of its right foot due to fifteen centuries of kissing.

The Three Degrees of Power

I got a kiss. Then I fell ill.
For cure another they advise me.
I got it. I am well. Now will
One more, I am sure, immortalize me.

—Greek song

Cherish Thy Spit

The ancient Chinese believed that there exist two holes under a woman's tongue which, if touched by a man's tongue during a kiss, release a magical transparent fluid called *Jade Spring* that is somehow beneficial to males. It is possible they were referring to saliva, since the "drinking" of it was advised in sixth-century B.C. Taoist philosophy.

It has since been discovered that saliva is indeed beneficial—to *all* mammals. It was noted in 1961 that lysozyme, a protein substance in saliva, suppresses infection and thereby encourages healing. Furthermore, a 1979 study conducted by four Australian doctors proved that other unidentified substances produced by salivary glands are major contributors to the healing process itself by effecting contraction of wounds. This was borne out by their experiments with mice, who "kiss" by licking each other's mouths in foreplay and, of course, lick their wounds as many mammals do.

The Australians said the next step would be to isolate the glands' mysterious healing element. Once that is done, perhaps the Japanese will manufacture it, the West will import it, and the Russians will steal it. Not to mention Rodeo Drive, which will make a killing on it. That leaves the poor American consumer, who will, undoubtedly, salivate over it. . . .

Kiss the Place to Make It Well

You cannot have forgotten the day already, when your life was endangered by the bite of a cientipedoro. The physician gave you over, declaring himself ignorant how to extract the venom. I knew but of one means, and hesitated not a moment to employ it. I was left alone with you; you slept; I loosened the bandage from your hand; I kissed the wound, and drew out the poison with my lips.

—Matthew Gregory Lewis, *The Monk*

Kiss Your Wife . . . and Stretch Your Life

A 1983 Italian publication reported a Peruvian doctor's finding that frequent kissing is closely associated with long life. This discovery supports a previous study conducted by a West German life insurance company, which concluded that a man who kisses his wife each morning before going to work will live five years longer than one who neglects such a display of affection.

The researchers also determined that those same men will be involved in fewer car accidents and gain 50 percent more usable time, due to a marked decrease in contracting disease.

The Secret Weapon

There is no woman who does not really desire, and who would not willingly permit, these kisses. Even the woman who has been chaste all her life; even the woman who, in the very climax of passion, still pursues that phantom, modesty; even such women will easily be brought to the point where they cannot forgo the pleasures of these "unchaste, unaesthetic" kisses, when once they have been fully and completely eroticized by means of them.

—Dr. Bernard Bauer, *Woman*

But Not Quite

When you kiss me, I almost faint.
—Clara Petacci
Excerpt from a letter to Benito Mussolini

Jaws 4-D—Winks, That Is

A kiss has the power to subdue a shark.

On Fiji Island, native fishermen catch sharks with their hands. They then flip the shark upside-down and kiss its belly. That kiss, for some unknown reason, has the effect of completely immobilizing the shark.

If only the heroes of *Jaws* had known this, it might have prevented all those unfortunate sequels!

Momma

Staying Power

Alas! that women do not know
Kisses make men loath to go.

—Anonymous

Learn and Multiply

"Deep kissing" was recommended as "a real antidote against depopulation" by Dr. Marcel Baudouin in an essay once presented to the Parisian Academie de Médecine. Dr. Baudouin was also a mayor in the Pays de Mont district of Vendée, Britanny, where the deep kiss was said to have been extremely popular among the Maraichins, people who lived in Marais, a marshy district in southern Vendée. Consequently, that intimate style of osculation was dubbed the Maraichinage.
Eventually the "French kiss" found its way to America. According to Kinsey, it is *least* utilized by adult males whose education does not exceed the eighth grade.

A Really Powerful Kiss

In fifteenth-century Italy, a kiss was considered to have the effect of partially deflowering a virginal woman.

By Mell Lazarus

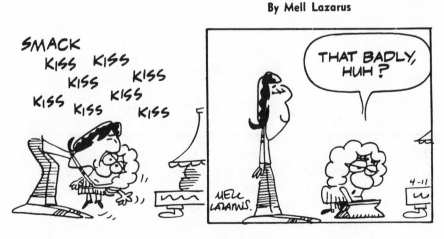

The kiss was very important in wedding ceremonies, especially if there were witnesses present. Once the kiss was passed, "the recipient was half-deflowered thereby." Any woman kissed in public and not subsequently married by the kisser was deemed forever unmarriageable, since no man in his right mind would marry a girl who was only 50 percent a virgin.

Instant Ownership

"Just because I kiss you—does that make me your girl?"
—Doris Day in *The Pajama Game* (Warner Brothers, 1957)

Make Yourself at Home

In certain Arabian tribes, a strategically placed kiss had the power to make a man a legal member of a family to whom he was not blood-related.

If a man was on the run from enemies who wished to kill him, he could save himself by taking refuge in the nearest tent and kissing the naked breasts of a woman inside. Such kisses automatically made that woman the fugitive's legal mother and, accordingly, all members of her family his relatives. He was henceforth afforded their protection and all the trappings of a real family.

A bizarre custom, perhaps, but the psychology behind it was simple: Kissing a woman's breasts is akin to sucking them, as the woman's child sucks. A parallel sentiment appears in the Song of Solomon (8:1): "O that thou wert as my brother, that sucked the breasts of my mother!"

Something to keep in mind, if you're ever on the run. . . .

Kiss and Break Up

A single kiss has the power to double a life span.

The organism known as paramecium has a reproductive system whereby a single protozoon will divide itself three hundred times before it dies. However, when two protozoa "kiss," connecting at their oral surfaces for a brief moment, the life span of each instantly doubles. In other words, they are "recharged" to the extent that another three hundred divisions are possible before their lives expire.

Some life forms get all the good breaks. . . .

The Metamorphosis

[When two people] kiss as lovers . . . a certain life-current passes through them which changes them forever.

—D. H. Lawrence

Please Stand By—This Is *Only* a Kiss

The next time your favorite TV show is disrupted by static interference, check outside. There may be some kissing going on.

That's what happened in England in 1953. In a documented case that ended up in the British courts, a Leicester man was watching TV when his picture suddenly became scrambled. He went outside his house and discovered that a young fellow was kissing his date good night inside his van while its motor maintained a fast idle. That engine was interfering with the local TV transmissions.

The kisser in the van immediately mistook the disgruntled TV viewer for a voyeur and wound up breaking the man's jaw. That about ruined the evening for TV watching *and* kissing—for both men.

Just an Expression

Never a lip is curved with pain
That can't be kissed into smiles again.

—Bret Harte, *The Lost Galleon*

 # 4. Six Kissing Mysteries

I wonder who's kissing her now?

—Frank R. Adams and Will M. Hough

The Case of the Middle East Mix-Up

The question of whether or not a kiss was passed between President Anwar Sadat of Egypt and Prime Minister Golda Meir of Israel was the key topic of Israeli controversy in November 1977.

Sadat arrived at Tel Aviv's Ben-Gurion Airport, approached the seventy-nine-year-old Mrs. Meir, and leaned forward to greet her. It was at this point that various onlookers thought they saw Sadat kiss her. As such a kiss would have been newsworthy, much checking was done by newsmen to verify what actually transpired.

Israeli reporter Zvi Zipper said, "We all saw Sadat lean over Mrs. Meir, pucker his lips, and kiss her." While neither Sadat nor Mrs. Meir was available to confirm or deny the reports, Golda's close friend Mrs. Lou Kedar claimed that "Mrs. Meir told me there was no kiss." No Egyptian witnesses to the kiss could be found, and the Israeli government out-and-out denied that any kiss took place.

The Case of the Impossible Kiss

No one has ever figured out how Russian movie director Sergei Komarov filmed the final kissing scene of his 1927 feature comedy, *Potselui Meri Pikford (The Kiss from Mary Pickford).*

Pretending to be a news cinematographer, Komarov had taken documentary footage of movie star Mary Pickford during her July 1926 visit to Moscow with Douglas Fairbanks. Without Miss Pickford's knowledge or consent, the scenes were later intercut with staged dramatic material to create a fictional story about a Russian movie extra intent on kissing the famous American actress. The film concludes with a happy ending in which the extra and Mary Pickford do indeed kiss. The orchestration of that kiss has forever remained a mystery.

The Case of the Mass Abstention

A 1939 Canadian "mass wedding," in which 105 couples were married at once, concluded before a crowd of 20,000 spectators with only one kiss.

The event had been organized by a group called the Young Catholic Workers as a publicity gimmick to help promote the institution of marriage in the face of an alleged increase in the international divorce rate.

However, no one could account for the fact that only one couple exchanged the betrothal kiss and 104 did not.

The Case of the Obstructive Parasol

The first kiss to take place in a Japanese movie may or may not have occurred behind an open parasol in Yasuki Chiba's 1946 film, *A Certain Night's Kiss*. (They had to invent a special word for "kiss," for correct Japanese has no such term.) The scene in question *implies* a kiss is about to occur, but a strategically placed parasol blocks the action. Only the actors themselves know for sure, but whatever they did behind that bumbershoot, it never made it onto celluloid.

Romantics may be offered hope in knowing that in Japan, parasols are considered a symbol of fertility by virtue of superstitions dating back to the fourth century.

The Case of the Mysterious Visitor

Edwin Booth was very shy about women. He tells of a harrowing experience that once befell him on a tour, when he had lain down to rest in his room and failed to lock his door:

"I heard a sound and opened my eyes. The door was being stealthily opened. I felt it was a woman. I couldn't move. She came in—the most determined woman I ever saw. She was tall, and gaunt, and strange. She couldn't help seeing I was trembling. She came to the bed, looked down upon me. Without smiling she bent over me—kissed me on the mouth. She didn't say a word. She walked out of the room. I never was so frightened in my life. I bolted the door when it was too late, but I'm not over it yet. I've tried to reason it out, but I can't. She was not silly. She looked to be the last woman on earth to care for kissing. I should say she was a hard woman."

—Edwin Fuller, *Literary Ancedotes*

The Case of the Crimson Kiss

Raymond Burr's eighth case in the series *Perry Mason* (CBS, 1957) found the famous lawyer having to solve a mystery involving a murdered playboy whose corpse had a lipstick imprint of a kiss on his forehead. In spite of the usual objections from the prosecution, Perry traced the kiss and won his case. The mystery, of course, still plagues us to this day—in reruns.

 5. The Cost of a Kiss

And I will have a lover's fee;
they say, unkiss'd unkind.
—George Peele, *Arraignement of Paris*

Hands Are Thai'd

Prison wardens in Bangkok, Thailand, have charged as much as $25 to visitors who wish to kiss their jailed spouses.

Momma

The practice first came to light in 1981 when an Australian woman, Gail Hayward, told a Melbourne newspaper that on two occasions she was required to pay a $25 fee to the warden of a Thai jail in order to kiss her husband, who had just begun to serve a twenty-year sentence for heroin smuggling.

Thai officials called the warden's kissing fee a "minor" offense that might warrant punishment, but not dismissal. Such "fee taking" is considered normal practice in many parts of the East.

To Kiss a Saint

In medieval Denmark, Catholic priests used to show a book containing illustrations of saints and allow parishioners to kiss the pictures for a fee. This fee was called kiss money. During the Reformation, this ritual was stopped, though voluntary offerings continued to be made.

Kiss and Sell

A new art form was created in 1979 when rock star David Bowie sent a "lipograph"—an autographed card bearing a lipstick imprint of his kiss—to a cosmetics firm publicist as a "thank you" gesture. Inspired by

By Mell Lazarus

the gift, the woman arranged for eighty celebrities to create their own lipographs to be auctioned off to the public as a charitable event for the Save the Children fund. Mick Jagger's kiss brought in $1,600, while Marlene Dietrich's smack pulled $1,200. By the time the buss bidders finished, London's Sotheby-Parke-Bernet had collected $16,000. (That's $200 a kiss, and all for the better.)

It Does a Body Good

Tony Curtis: Where did you learn to kiss like that?
Marilyn Monroe: I used to sell kisses for the milk fund.
Curtis: Tomorrow, remind me to send a check for $100,000 to the milk fund.

—*Some Like It Hot* (United Artist/Mirisch, 1959)

Token Kiss a Real Money Raiser

Certain preteens in Manhattan "kiss" subway turnstyles—not out of reverence or homage but pure greed.

A kid stuffs turnstyle slots with cardboard, blocking up the mechanism that receives passengers' tokens. The culprit then steps back and waits. When a commuter inserts a token, it is prevented from dropping by the cardboard. The youth then puckers up, gives the slot a smack, and sucks out the stuck token, which he sells for cash. Police say that a single kid may pull as many as a hundred such criminal kisses in one day, netting him a cool $90.00.

Yankees Passed the Buck?

These days, people in need of borrowing a dime do so to make a phone call or to buy time on a parking meter. Many years ago, however, a guy who asked a lady for a dime hoped to get a kiss.

A "Yankee dime" was a slang term used primarily in the southern United States to signify "payment in full by a kiss." A "Quaker nickel" sometimes was taken to mean the same and a "Dutch quarter" denoted a hug.

Presumably 30¢ or 35¢ got you both.

A Kiss Preserved

A memento of a 1932 kiss from Greta Garbo is worth $1,575. That's the price that was paid in 1980 for a faded yellow rose the famous actress once kissed.

Photographer Cecil Beaton had met Garbo at a party in 1932 and fell in love with her. She later pulled a rose from a vase, kissed it, and handed it to Beaton, telling him, "A rose lives and dies and never returns again." Though Garbo turned down a marriage proposal from Beaton, he treasured the rose for the rest of his life.

Enamored by the romantic story, another photographer, Gary Rogers, purchased the preserved flower at an auction held following Beaton's death—some forty-eight years after that Garbo kiss.

Glove and Kisses

We have seen how stolen gloves could win a New England man a kiss from the owner for their return. Contrariwise, any New England girl who wanted a new pair of gloves could acquire them by kissing a man while he slept. Then, too, a newly married Yankee couple could raise money from wedding guests by auctioning off a pair of decorated gloves. The successful bidder would then cash in his prize by exchanging the gloves for a kiss from the bride.

Must have been excellent times for the glove industry.

Credit Is Good

Give me kisses! Nay, 'tis true
I am just as rich as you;
And for every kiss I owe
I can pay you back, you know.
Kiss me, then,
Every moment—and again.

—John Godfrey Saxe

Prescriptions Eagerly Filled

Good-night kisses from fraternity men could be purchased by coeds at the University of Connecticut in 1980. For a fee of 99¢ the Kappi Psi pharmaceutical students would, in P.J.s, visit a woman at her dorm and deliver the kiss—if desired—after a dramatic reading of a bedtime story, such as "Sleeping Beauty." Teddy bears were also provided.

Smooch 'n' Smuggle

The kisses of a group of Bronx women were responsible, in 1981, for raising over $10 million—all of it from prison inmates.

The money-making kisses were part of an elaborate narcotics operation in which the ladies visited prisoners at Rikers Island and the Bronx House of Detention and passed the men drug-filled balloons via their kisses. The inmates then sold the heroin, marijuana, and cocaine to other prisoners on the inside.

The drug ring was busted on August 19, 1981, when thirty-one people were arrested for operating the smooch-'n'-smuggle caper.

That'll Teach Them

Students of Sunset High School in Miami, Florida, paid to see their teachers kiss a pig as part of a 1982 fund-raiser.

The pig wasn't sure, but he figured he must've done *something* right.

The Jane Fonda Kissing Workout

How much can it cost a movie studio to have two superstars kiss in a motion picture? Would you believe $280,000?

That was what Columbia Pictures reportedly forked out for Jane Fonda and Robert Redford to connect lips in the 1979 production *The Electric Horseman*. Hollywood sources report that that particular kissing scene required forty-eight separate takes over a period of two days. Sex symbols don't come cheap—and neither do their kisses!

The Glory of Debits

The kiss you take is paid by that you give:
The joy is mutual, and I'm still in debt.
—George Granville, *Heroic Love*

To Kiss or Not to Kiss

 1. Excuses, Excuses

"I hadn't kissed anyone when I got married, heavens to God, no. Nor afterwards either; I always thought it was a revolting habit."
—Alice Roosevelt Longworth, quoted in
The First Time by Karl Fleming and Anne Taylor Fleming

Holy Admonishment

Kissing was long forbidden among orthodox Jews, even between husband and wife. The Talmud described the practice as unhealthy, and permitted a married couple only those actions directly related to the sex act itself. In time many of these rules of morality were adopted in modified forms by the Christian religion.

Sip of the Lip

Our vicar he calls it damnation to sip
The ripe ruddy dew of a woman's dear lip.
—Sir Walter Scott

A Heavyweight Promise

Heavyweight boxing champ Muhammed Ali appeared at a 1979 Los Angeles press conference to promote a TV movie he was starring in. Seated in front of a photo blowup of himself, Ali, a devout Muslim, preached "the spirit of Allah" in vowing never to act in a production that entailed "kissing women." And I'll bet there hasn't been a producer yet who's put up a fight about it.

Have Kiss, Will Travel

An Anti-Kissing League was formed in Mexico City in 1904 for the purpose of making the public trolley system operate more efficiently.

An all-female group boasting a membership of three hundred, the league believed that a self-imposed ban on good-bye kisses at all trolley stops would keep the trolleys from running late. Each AKL member, on joining, took a solemn pledge never to kiss any other member of the league, either in public *or* private. There was no explanation as to how banning kissing between women behind closed doors would improve trolley time, though the league was also concerned about contagious diseases and possibly promoted the privacy rule for health reasons.

The potential problem of league members not recognizing one another—on trolleys or otherwise—was solved with red ID buttons, which all Anti-Kissers wore on their blouses or jackets.

Public reaction to the AKL was perhaps summed up in a November 20 newspaper editorial, which said that "the [League's] practice . . . is decidedly, to the male sense, not only deplorable, but unnecessary. . . . How far this new League will conduct its offensive and defensive campaign remains to be seen."

Clean and Kissless

In Finland, mouth-to-mouth kissing was always considered obscene, yet mixed bathing in the nude was quite common. Nonetheless, the Finns do have a term for kissing: *antaa sunta*. Translation: "to give mouth."

Tell Her to Dry Up

1. "I'd love to kiss you, but I just washed my hair."
   —Bette Davis to Richard Barthelmess in
   Cabin in the Cotton (Warner Brothers, 1932)

2. Theda Bara just washed her hair, but kissed her man anyway—at the end of her wedding ceremony.

In 1921, the Hollywood vamp drove to Connecticut with her fiancé, director Charles Brabin, to get married. "Neither of us had ever been on time in our lives," recalled Bara, "so I thought, 'I'll shampoo my hair.'" That she did and found herself dripping wet at her own wedding. "I had to stick up my wet hair under my picture hat," she explained, "and I sneezed throughout the ceremony." But, unlike Bette Davis' film character, Theda did *not* use her predicament as an excuse to avoid kissing—or marrying.

Off-the-Wall Advice

Young ladies: You shouldn't go strolling about
When your anxious mammas don't know you are out;
And remember that accidents often befall
From kissing young fellows through holes in the wall.
       —John Godfrey Saxe, "Pyramus and Thisbe: Moral"

Carryed Away

Any couple kissing inside a carriage parked on a public street in Kansas at the turn of the century was setting the stage for an attack by an umbrella-wielding harridan, temperance reformer Carry A. Nation. It is not known if amorous neckers were actually stabbed with Mrs. Nation's formidable weapon, but its brandishment certainly underscored the seriousness of her accompanying verbal onslaught. Sometimes, however, she tried the preventive route by accosting lone women on the street and imploring them to resist the osculatory and sexual advances of all men.

The act of kissing indeed became a risky practice—even more so when Carry later traded in her umbrella for a hatchet.

Thank Goodness Fashions Come and Go

It is not a fashion for the maids in France to kiss before they are married.
       —William Shakespeare, *Henry V*

The Samoan View

Samoan girls are said to "look upon kissing with disgust," according to Australian George Lewis Becke's *Pacific Tales*. (Notice he didn't say they they don't like doing it; they just don't like to *look* at it.)

The Things He Did for U.N.C.L.E.

Dedicated fans of a popular TV series made an impassioned plea to the show's producers in 1965, requesting that one of its stars—a teen heartthrob—refrain from kissing in any future episodes.

The series was MGM's *The Man From U.N.C.L.E.,* and the star was a sexy blond Scot, David McCallum. McCallum portrayed a Russian, Illya Kuryakin, who worked as a top agent for the secret global law enforcement network that was in constant battle against THRUSH, a ubiquitous and sinister conspiracy out to subjugate all humanity. With his Beatle-length haircut, romantic "Russian" accent, and black turtleneck attire, McCallum rapidly became the idol of teenage girls everywhere. So much so, that his occasional romantic interludes on the series set female blood aboiling.

In "The Bow-Wow Affair" episode, David—as Illya—hides in some bushes with actress Susan Oliver, who takes advantage of the opportunity to request a kiss. "Well certainly, if you insist," replies Illya. And they do. Meanwhile, David's fans were overcome with jealousy. Three in particular, students at Wellesley College, fired off letters to both McCallum and executive producer Norman Felton.

To David, they begged, "Please, no more kissing. You will destroy your image with us." And to Felton: "If you hire anyone as a romantic lead opposite Illya Kuryakin, MGM studios and every TV set tuned to *U.N.C.L.E.* will be blown to smithereens and all Wellesley students will double-cross U.N.C.L.E. for THRUSH."

The college girls soon received a personal response from McCallum, obviously cleared and forwarded via Section IV of U.N.C.L.E.'s New York headquarters: "My faithful comrades in arms: Certain subversive THRUSH agents can only be uncovered by a variety of experiences. . . . Regret no man is perfect. (Signed) Illya Kuryakin."

The girls must have bought it, for Illya continued to kiss off THRUSH baddies for another three years before U.N.C.L.E. was finally done in by an even more powerful conspiracy, NBC.

In Love and Politics

"Don't tell me it's subversive to kiss a Republican."
—John Lund to Congresswoman Jean Arthur in
A Foreign Affair (Paramount, 1948)

From Russia with Kisses

During the early twentieth century, the Central Committee of the Young Communist Organization of Saratov, Russia, orchestrated a hysterical campaign against kissing. They distributed leaflets attacking the practice as "a sinister . . . sign of social disintegration disgraceful for a society of class-conscious workers and peasants."

The campaign never quite gained popular or official support, a fact that was then explored in an article by Moscow satirist A. Soritch:

"So, the kiss poisons the righteous mind of a revolutionist and paralyzes his will in the battle for communism! . . . Are kisses in general to be abolished under Order No. 722? . . . or only the evening kisses under the chestnut tree. . . ? Are brotherly kisses upon the earlobes or the nose allowed? Are kisses permissible when preceded by a Marxian analysis of the causes and waves of feeling from which this custom arises. . . ?

"One . . . made the not so unreasonable suggestion that the number of kisses be rationed out on a descending scale. Say a daily portion of five kisses in the beginning, which would be lessened by one kiss at every anniversary of the revolution. . . .

"Strange to say, thus far this burning question has never been made the subject of a single circular from Moscow, nor of a leading editorial in *Pravda*, nor of even the thinnest kind of a brochure in the Party libraries. . . .

"But why wait for Moscow? Perhaps the people there have not grasped the importance of this matter. . . ."

In time, they did. Public kissing is now viewed, in the Soviet Union, as highly improper, and those caught doing it are quickly called to task. Today, an A. Soritch would unfortunately be much less likely to get away with such a critique, tongue in cheek or not.

Campaign Promise

Political baby kissing must come to an end, unless the size and the age of the babies be materially increased.

—W. C. Fields

He Shouldn't Have Asked

Why do I not kiss you, Philaenis? You are bald, you are carrotty, you are one-eyed. He who kisses you sins against nature.

—Martial, *Epigrams*

Even in Faraway Galaxies

"I'd just as soon kiss a Wookie."
—Carrie Fisher rebuffing Harrison Ford, in
The Empire Strikes Back (Fox, 1980)

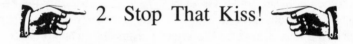 2. Stop That Kiss!

Here's to fanatics, who constantly try
To put something over to keep us all dry;
A law they'll soon pass that a crime you commit
If you kiss your own wife without a permit.

—Anonymous

Of Kisses and Lives—Publicly Executed

Many countries have maintained strict laws against kissing in public.

Kuwait introduced such an ordinance following a celebrated 1974 case in which two minors were arrested after they kissed in the street. Saudi Arabia's special police will haul in public kissers in order to prevent the spread of immorality.

In ancient Greece, those who kissed in the open were simply put to death. Perhaps it was this law, more than jealousy, that motivated Greek men to insist that their wives eat onions before leaving home alone.

Pietro Lando, sixteenth-century doge of Padua, had his own son beheaded for kissing a girl in public. Even in early America, public neckers had those necks put on more permanent display in a wooden pillory.

Today, consulting firms offer special programs designed to inform business travelers of the various laws and customs of different countries so that ignorant souls don't get put before a firing squad for passing kisses that may very well constitute a capital crime.

Kissing up to Khomeini

A hundred lashes is the penalty for kissing in Iran. Any kiss is criminal, whether done in public or private, provided its purpose is to produce sexual pleasure.

The law, which was passed by the Islamic Parliament in 1982, states that kissing offenses must be proved by either four male or two female witnesses.

Iranian kisses of worship, however, are perfectly legal—unless practiced in Saudi Arabia. In 1981, two Iranians were imprisoned for kissing the tomb of Muhammad, a Shi'ite Muslim ritual opposed by Arabia's Sunni Muslims.

The rule of the Ayatollah Khomeini is responsible for a full list of moral crimes recently added to Iranian statute books. The kissing ban was such a hit that, three months after its establishment, the government of Malaysia (an Islamic country) decided to outlaw kissing too, as part of a new policy "to expose elements of Islamic law to the people."

These countries are right in line with seventeenth-century New England, where Boston judges could order a man whipped or jailed as punishment for kissing a girl he was courting.

Alive and Well in America

The state of kissing in the United States today is generally well known: it is a far cry from our liberality to the old Blue Laws of Connecticut, with a heavy penalty for kissing one's wife on Sundays or fast days, and, for all we know, boiling in oil for kissing the wife of another. It is still unlawful to kiss a girl against her will: the courts awarding damages to the girl varying from $750 in Pennsylvania and $2,500 in New York, to $1.15 in New Jersey. And while there are Anti-Osculation Leagues, with stern medical warnings of the danger of kissing, the custom shows no evidence of diminution.

—Clement Wood, "The Art of Kissing"

Kissing in the Fast Lane

The daughter of the Duke of Rutland was recently fined $112 for kissing an interior decorator—while driving her car in the fast lane of a British expressway.

Lady Teresa Manners, age twenty, was said to have been "totally oblivious to other traffic" as she embraced her passenger, Malcolm Connell, during a two-mile stretch of highway in Coleshill, England, in 1983.

Connell was also fined—as an accessory to the kiss.

A Real Buss Stop

A train station in Deerfield, Illinois, features special zones—located fifty feet apart—for both *Kissing* and *No Kissing*. Each zone is designated by a sign showing the silhouette of a woman in curlers kissing a man in a hat, the *No* sign bearing a red slash across the image.

"Wives, still in bathrobe and curlers, drive their husbands to the train so they can go to their jobs downtown," explained a Deerfield official. "But traffic was always blocked while the couples kissed each other good-bye. This way, they can pull to the side to kiss."

Some couples obey the signs, others do not. "When the government starts telling me where I can kiss my wife, that's when I become a lawbreaker," said one commuter.

Two signs at the Deerfield, Illinois, train station to keep kissers from disrupting commuter traffic. © 1979 by Village of Deerfield, Illinois

"Of course, you can't enforce it," assured assistant village manager Marge Emery. "It's just a joke—a whimsical method of keeping the traffic moving."

The signs have nonetheless created controversy in the Chicago suburb. "We got a nasty letter from a university student," said a Chamber of Commerce representative. "She must've been part of the women's movement, because she was upset that the signs show the man in a hat and the woman in curlers. But that's usually the way it is. . . ."

You Aren't What You Wear

During a church service in thirteenth-century France, a kiss was passed that resulted in the implementation of a national dress code.

Among the members of this particular congregation was Queen Marguerite, consort of Louis IX. When the pastor called for everyone to exchange the kiss of peace, the queen eyed a well-dressed woman and kissed her. It later came to light that the lady the queen had bussed was a mere commoner, not the aristocrat suggested by her mode of attire. Infuriated over this "deception," the queen complained to the king, who quickly enacted a law governing public dress. Never again would her majesty be subjected to such humiliation!

Closely Watched Wives

There used to exist laws designed to prevent a man's wife from kissing any other man. In medieval France, a married woman who violated that law was found guilty of adultery. Among the Welsh, a husband who caught his wife kissing another male—even as a greeting—had the legal right to expel her from his home forever. The laws may have eased since those days, but the rage in the heart of a jealous lover—male *or* female— can still be as fierce as ever.

Her Kisses Belonged to Daddy

Did you ever see a movie featuring a kissing scene with actress Evelyn Venable? Her father certainly hopes not. When Paramount Pictures signed Ms. Venable to a studio contract in 1933, he insisted that a clause be inserted forbidding his daughter to do any on-screen smooching. This filmic bit of trivia surfaced in a Guinness Records book, Patrick Robertson's *Movie Facts and Feats*.

Burt Lancaster and Deborah Kerr in *From Here to Eternity*, 1953

Beach Blanket Blues

On May 14, 1914, the city commissioners of Long Beach, California adopted a measure for the purpose of protecting the morals of the city's youth. The antispooning ordinance, as it was called, forbade kissing in any "park, avenue, street, court, way, alley . . . or the beach." It also made it a crime for a boy to rest his head on a girl's lap, especially when garbed in bathing suits. The penalty for violation was a fine and/or imprisonment. "No public manifestations of sentiment will be tolerated in any degree," warned the council. One would guess that *private* manifestations quickly became all the rage.

The Kissers' Rebellion of '69

The turbulent 1960s are well-remembered for youthful rebellion— protests, marches, sit-ins, and clashes with police. Most of it was related to civil rights and antiwar sentiment. But not all. One little-known rebellion occurred over kissing.

The place was Majorca, Spain. The year, 1969. In the town of Inca, the chief of police found himself faced with a difficult problem: Young lovers would regularly engage in unabashed public kissing. The solution, the chief decided, was to hand out citations, fining the kissers 500 pesetas (about $7) per kiss.

The kissers were outraged by this and organized a mass protest. Thirty couples assembled for a "kiss-in" at the Figuera Harbor and, in blatant defiance of the law, kissed away to their hearts' content. The police chief immediately plunged into action and orchestrated a massive roundup of the lawless neckers. The amorous rebels were hauled in to the slammer, allowed to cool off, and fined 45,000 pesetas prior to release.

Nothing like a little law and order to cool off hot—lips.

Roll 'Em!

That twentieth-century phenomenon, necking in a darkened movie theater, was almost outlawed in Italy. A 1953 court case in Naples sought to determine if the kisses exchanged between a student and his girlfriend in a local cinema house were obscene and therefore criminal. After endless appeals, the highest court finally ruled in favor of the movie-going kissers. All the better for young romantics—*and* the film biz!

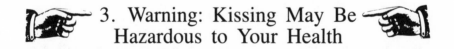

3. Warning: Kissing May Be Hazardous to Your Health

> They say there's microbes in a kiss,
> This rumor is most rife,
> Come, lady dear, and make of me
> An invalid for life.
>
> —Anonymous

Kissing with Glass

As many as 278 *colonies* of bacteria can be passed from one person to another during a kiss. This figure was the result of a scientific kissing experiment conducted by male and female students at Baltimore's City College in the late 1950s. The outcome of the experiment was nothing to get sick over: the students had kissed glass slides rather than each other. And besides that, the results also showed that 95 percent of the transmitted colonies are completely harmless.

Who's Counting?

Every kiss we take and give
Leaves us less of life to live.

—Anonymous

The Kissing Diet

Scarsdale, Weight-Watchers, Macrobiotic, Beverly Hills, James Coco, and Pritikin—eat your heart out! *The Kissing Diet* has arrived!

Kisses—lots and lots of kisses—may well be the key to effective weight loss. This is according to psychologist Hans Ziegler, who presented his finding in *New Behavior* magazine. Ziegler claimed that the ideal way to avoid casual munching is to replace food with kisses. (Preferably, kisses *not* made of chocolate.)

Indeed, the way to a man's (or woman's) stomach is through the heart!

Henpecks

I get no respect from my wife. She kisses the dog, but she won't drink out of my glass.

—Rodney Dangerfield

Those Creepy Bedtime Kissers

The "kissing bug" is a blood-sucking insect that thrives in lawns and in the coats of dogs and rats. During the bite of a kissing bug, a liquid created by the insect is injected into the host to replace the blood that is sucked out. The bite of certain varieties of kissing bug can transmit a flagellate, *Trypanosoma cruzi*, which causes Chagas' disease, a virulent tropical fever.

Except for its mosquitolike sting, kissing bugs do not "kiss." The black insect, whose scientific name is *Triatoma protracta*, was dubbed the kissing bug at the turn of the century when a rumor started that an insect was killing people by biting them on the lips. The .06-inch-long North American variety, *Melanolestes picipes*, does have a preference for the human face, while conenosed *Triatoma*—found usually in the Southwest and in South and Central America—is reportedly less picky.

Reach out and Kiss Someone

Mononucleosis has long been known as the kissing disease because the illness can be transferred through kisses. Infected blood cells of the mouth are also able to carry transmittable antigens, which can—via kissing—spread hepatitis virus to those susceptible to it, just as contaminated blood transfusions or hypodermic needles can.

Herpes I, a virus that results in oral cold sores, is a frequent passenger among kisses, and has perhaps replaced mono as the most-discussed "lover's leach." In fact, a Foster City, California, waitress who set up a kissing booth in 1983 was forced to substitute chocolate kisses for the ones she was unable to give away by mouth, due to the widespread fear of herpes.

The majority of the adult American population has at some time been infected with herpes I, yet many may not know it. The virus often remains in seclusion, only to surface as cold sores during stressful or biologically disruptive times of life. Until the medical community finds a cure, stay calm—and kiss in good health.

Laying on the Lip-Shtick

A woman's lipstick may be helpful in preventing transference of germs during a kiss. This theory was put forth by *Woman* magazine in its advice to a reader who complained that her boyfriend refused to kiss her while she wore makeup. *Woman* told the girl to explain to her lover that the antiseptic properties of lipstick would "suffocate the colonies of bacteria transferred when two people kiss."

If true, women must battle an awful lot of germs, since the average female uses about ten times her height in lipstick during her entire lifetime. Kind of makes a fellow reflect on how much lipstick he's been smeared with in his *own* lifetime.

One gentleman from Deer Park, New York, would probably prefer *not*

During a 1937 Flu Epidemic, Hollywood donned antiseptic masks during rehearsal of kissing scenes.

to think about it. In 1981, Robert Stevens was literally enveloped in lipstick but didn't even get the benefit of a kiss along with it. A giant vat of 240-degree molten lipstick overturned onto the cosmetics factory worker in a freak accident, leaving Stevens severely burned.

Just a cool touch of the stuff from a lady's lips will do nicely, thank you.

Saturday Night Massacre

Too passionate a kiss can result in temporomandibular dysfunction—that is, impairment of the joint between the jawbone (mandible) and the temporal bone at the side and base of the skull. So says Dr. George A. Zarb, University of Toronto dentist. Dr. Zarb has claimed that heavy necking can produce such a strain on kissers that their jawbones may become sore or immobilized, resulting in an inability to chew hard food. He tagged the phenomenon the Saturday Night Syndrome, because patients so often turned up at the dental clinic on Monday morning with the same symptoms. So bad can the syndrome be that one young woman's problem was diagnosed by her doctor—based on X rays—as a whiplash injury, and described by the physician as one of the strangest cases he'd ever seen.

Kisses from Camelot

Dave Powers, Kennedy family friend, once said that John F. Kennedy, during an early congressional campaign, "kissed more babies than the nine candidates put together." And what did JFK himself have to say about the practice? "Kissing babies," admitted Kennedy, "gives me asthma." No wonder.

A Real Drag

Kissing a smoker is like licking a dirty ashtray.

—Anonymous

Brush After Every Kiss

1. A man who will kiss a pretty girl's lips passionately, may perhaps be disgusted at the idea of using her toothbrush.

—Anonymous

2. Kisses are leading transmitters of germs that cause dental disease, according to Dr. Paul H. Keyes of the National Institute of Dental Research. Keyes has claimed that cavities and various gum problems can be communicated between people who kiss. For that reason, he recommended that relatives and romantic partners of diseased patients be examined with extra care.

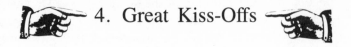

4. Great Kiss-Offs

> It should be my wishing,
> That I might die with kissing.
>
> —Ben Jonson

Tarzan's Last Call

Johnny Weissmuller, cinema's most famous Tarzan, kissed his wife, Maria, as a final gesture immediately before he passed away in 1984. Daughter Lisa recalled, "When Mom went in to say good night, he grabbed her and gave her a kiss. . . . A couple of minutes later he died."

The Final Kiss

In the past, people whose religious convictions included belief in the hereafter would kiss the mouths of the dying in order to trap and preserve the departing spirit. This practice originated with the Italians. Earlier, during the sixth century, certain societies prohibited any kissing of the body after death. A current Greek funeral rite calls for the mourners to kiss only the coffin.

The Kiss We Shared

The ring was all blood-stained . . . so I put the ring on Jack's finger . . . and then I kissed his hand. . . .
> —Jacqueline Kennedy, recalling the moments
> after her husband's death, November 1963

The Kindest Exit

Religious lore often depicts the death of sainted persons as a result of a kiss from God. It is said that Saint Monica died after being kissed on her breast by a child. The Hebrews viewed death in this light—the metaphor later adopted by the Italians in a saying, "To fall asleep in the Lord's kiss."

A Kiss Abused

Sing me dead, caress me dead,
Kiss away the curse of living.

—Heinrich Heine

By Death Deprived

My lips are so paralysed that they could not kiss—and it is harder to do without kissing than without speaking.

—Heinrich Heine

Hanging on to Dear Wife

A very old Moscow magazine reported a story about a jealous, elderly Russian peasant who, on his deathbed, asked his young wife to bestow a final kiss on his lips. As she obliged, her dying husband suddenly sank his teeth deep into her lips, his intention being to mutilate her so that she'd be rendered unkissable and, consequently, an unlikely candidate for remarriage after his death. So tightly was she imprisoned by the dead man's vicious kiss that a knife finally had to be employed to release her.

Doctor Prescribed Kiss After Death

The 1910 suicide in France of Russian medical student Tania Rachevskaya led to a unique request by her former lover. The man, a Romanian doctor, was a fellow countryman of famed sculptor Constantin Brancuşi, who had recently completed his pioneer work, *The Kiss*. The doctor asked that the abstract sculpture be placed on Tania's tombstone in the Montparnesse Cemetery of Paris, and Brancuşi obliged. Its installation there reportedly shocked many people of the time. Nearly half a century later, Brancuşi himself was buried in the very same cemetery.

Brancusi's *The Kiss*

"Thus with a Kiss I Die"

I will kiss thy lips.
Haply some poison yet doth hang on them
To make me die. . . .

—The bereaved Juliet to the poisoned Romeo
William Shakespeare, *Romeo and Juliet*

The Kiss That Killed a King

The kiss of a ten-year-old girl was said to have killed Louis XV.

The king was traveling by carriage across country when he pulled over to greet a farmer's young daughter, who was standing by the roadside. Louis pinched her cheek, but she was unusually quiet. The king then kissed her and departed. He died shortly thereafter, having contracted smallpox from the girl by way of the kiss.

Rolling a Pair of Snake Lips

One of the daring stunts performed by snake handlers in Texas' annual National Rattlesnake Championship is called "the kiss of death." As its title suggests, the stunt features a handler touching his lips to those of a cobra—probably devenomed.

A similar feat was performed in a major motion picture by actress Barbara Carrera, self-proclaimed sufferer from ophidiophobia (morbid fear of snakes). As a wicked assassin in the movie *Never Say Never Again* (Warner Brothers, 1983), the Nicaraguan beauty was to exchange kisses with another Latin beauty, a live (though nonpoisonous) boa constrictor—while driving a car yet.

"They didn't tell me about the snake until I was in too deep," she later told an interviewer. "I caressed it, put it around my neck and let it crawl all over my body. . . . Then I let it kiss me on the cheek with its little, darting tongue. I think I even kissed *it*, too!"

Some snakes have all the luck.

Think Before You Kiss

Mayhem, death and arson
Have followed many a thoughtless kiss
Not sanctioned by a parson.

—Don Marquis, "On Kissing"

You *Can* Take Them with You

The kissing of the *tali* before death was an important part of Hindu suttee rituals.

What began as a deterrent against wives murdering their husbands—once very common in India—eventually developed into a religious custom. Following the death of her husband, a woman would join her mate's corpse on its funeral pyre and be burned alive in a public ceremony. However, before the pyre was lighted, the widow would quietly kiss the *tali*, a jeweled amulet given to her by her husband on their wedding day.

The Vampire's Kiss

CHAPTER EIGHT

The Joy of Kissing

 1. Love and Kisses

How delicious is the winning
Of a kiss at Love's beginning.
—Thomas Campbell, "Song"

The Kiss of His Dreams

Tansey flew to Katie, and took her in his arms like a conquering knight. She raised her face, and he kissed her—violets! electricity! caramels! champagne! Here was the attainment of a dream that brought no disenchantment.

—O. Henry

The Kiss Conditional

A kiss is nothing if the heart be mute.
—French proverb

Kisses Beget Kisses

If you're not getting any kisses from the person you love, or if the love itself is gone, one cure might be more kisses. *Chocolate* kisses.

———— 149 ————

A study conducted by the New York State Psychiatric Institute claims that phenylethylamine, a chemical present in both the human brain *and* chocolate, is responsible for the emotional high experienced when one is "in love." The brain halts output of the chemical when one becomes depressed, but the love state may be restored by the consumption of chocolate.

Good excuse, isn't it?

Take It with a Grain of Salt

They hugged each other very tightly, exchanging kisses rendered surpassingly salty by their tears. This is thought by some to add relish, as with peanuts, by bringing out the sweetness.

—John Collier

Pas de Deux

In love, there is always one who kisses and one who offers the cheek.

—French proverb

Request of the Miller's Daughter

When I was a young man I had a mistress, a miller's daughter, whom I used to see when I went out hunting. She would never accept anything from me. One day, however, she said to me, "You must bring me a present." "What do you want?" "Bring me a bar of soap." When I did so, she disappeared, came back covered with blushes, held out her scented hands and said, "Now kiss my hands as you kiss the hands of the ladies in the drawing room of St. Petersburg."

I threw myself on my knees before her.

—Ivan Turgenev

A Bird in the Hand

Here's to the man who kisses his sweetheart
And kisses his sweetheart alone,
For many a man kisses another man's sweetheart
When he thinks he's kissing his own.

—Anonymous

Beyond the Cup

1. First take the cup and kiss the very place
Which with her lips she did in drinking grace.
—Ovid, *Ars Amatoria*

2. Eighteenth-century novelist and philosopher Jean-Jacques Rousseau went way beyond Ovid's suggested cup in kissing the objects touched by the woman *he* loved. Indeed, Rousseau set his lips upon floors, chairs, curtains—and even a petticoat (while it was empty, of course).

How About Sleep?

If kissing were the only joy in bed,
One woman would another woman wed.
—Anonymous

Of Pillows and Kisses

I can't get that fascinating picture of you in the midst of the pillows of the "big, low, old-timey bed" out of my head, or the longing out of my heart to stoop over you there and take you in my arms and cover you with kisses.

—President Woodrow Wilson
Letter to Edith Bolling Galt

For Better or Worse

1. After kissing comes more kindness.
—John Clarke, *Paroemiologia*
2. She that will kiss, they say, will do worse.
—Robert Davenport, *City Night Cap*

Straight, Dry, and Breathless

Suddenly she went up to him and put her hand through his arm. "Kiss me," she said; "I am going to belong to you."
"Jean!"

"No, Hubert, no chivalry and that sort of nonsense. You shan't have all this beastliness alone. I'm going to share it. Kiss me."

The kiss was given. It was long, and soothing to them both; but, when it was over, he said:

"Jean, it's quite impossible till things dry straight."

"Of course they'll dry straight, but I want to help dry them. Let's be married quickly, Hubert. Father can spare me a hundred a year; what can you manage?"

"I've three hundred a year of my own, and half pay, which may be cut off."

"That's four hundred a year certain; people have married on lots less, and that's only for the moment. Of course we can be married. Where?"

Hubert stood breathless.

"When the war was on," said Jean, "people married at once; they didn't wait because the man was going to be killed. Kiss me again."

And Hubert stood more breathless than ever. . . .

—John Galsworthy, *Maid in Waiting*

A Kiss Received

I promised everything for a kiss. It is true that, having taken the kiss, I did not keep my promise; but I had good reasons. Had we agreed that it should be taken or given? After much bargaining, we agreed on a second, and it was said that this should be received. Then I guided the timid arms around my body, I held her more amorously in one of mine, and the soft kiss was indeed received, well received, perfectly received, in short, love himself could not have done better.

—Pierre Choderlos de Laclos, *Liaisons Dangereux*

Second-Degree Burn

The offering of kisses was classified as the second "degree" of love by André le Chapelain in 1176. The French writer asserted that "throughout all the ages, there have been only four degrees of love," of which kissing ranks second. The first is "arousing hope," the third is "enjoyment of intimate embraces," and last is "the abandonment of the entire person."

All or Nothing

A loving kiss can never be chaste; the two things are incompatible. To love platonically and to kiss is as absurd as a hunger striker who would carry out his purpose by becoming a vegetarian.

—Herbert Bauer

Message to Mankind

Hang up love's mistletoe over the earth,
And let us kiss under it all the year round.

—Anonymous

 Six Kisses That Bombed

"There's something terribly uncomplimentary in apologizing for kissing a beautiful woman."

—Richard Arlen to Ida Lupino in
Artists and Models (Paramount, 1937)

Kisses Impossible

It was very little that Nicholas knew of the world, but he guessed enough about its ways to think that if he gave Miss La Creevy one little kiss, perhaps she might not be the less kindly disposed towards those he was leaving behind. So he gave her three or four with a kind of jocose gallantry, and Miss La Creevy evinced no greater symptoms of displeasure than declaring, as she adjusted her yellow turban, that she had never heard of such a thing, and couldn't have believed it possible.

—Charles Dickens, *Nicholas Nickleby*

Her Feet Were Cold and Fast

The betrothal kiss marks the end of the wedding ceremony and the beginning of married life for the bridal couple. But for Mehran Derakhshan, that kiss may have ushered in the shortest marriage on record: *two minutes*.

No sooner had her 1980 London ceremony ended, than twenty-two-year-old Denis Mathew complained of a headache and walked out on her husband. Mehran was granted a legal divorce two years later.

The Shiver

He tilted her head farther back, bending his own down until his lips were nearly touching hers. She shivered involuntarily, an anguished appeal leaping into her eyes. He smiled ironically. "Do you hate them so much, my kisses?"

She swallowed convulsively.

"You are at least candid if you are not complimentary;" and with that he released her and turned away.

—E. M. Hull, *The Sheik*

A Barrel of Kisses

"It made me sick when I had to let you kiss me. I only did it because you begged me. You hounded me. You drove me crazy. And, after you kissed me, I always used to wipe my mouth—*wipe my mouth*—but I made up for it. For every kiss, I had to laugh."

—Bette Davis to Leslie Howard
Of Human Bondage (RKO, 1934)

One Kiss Too Many

My cheek reclined on her shoulder—kissing her hands by turns. Rather bashfully then angrily reluctant, her hands sought to be withdrawn; her shoulder avoiding my reclined cheek—apparently loath, and more loath, to quarrel with me; her downcast eye confessing more than her lips could utter. Now surely, thought I, is my time to try if she can forgive a still bolder freedom than I had ever yet taken.

I then gave her struggling hands liberty. I put one arm round her waist: I imprinted a kiss on her sweet lips, with a *Be quiet* only, and an averted face, as if she feared another.

Encouraged by so gentle a repulse, the tenderest things I said; and then, with my other hand, drew aside the handkerchief that concealed the beauty of beauties, and pressed with my burning lips the most charming breast that ever my ravished eyes beheld.

A very contrary passion to that which gave her bosom so delightful a swell immediately took place. She struggled out of my encircling arms with indignation. I detained her reluctant hand. Let me go, said she. *I see there is no keeping terms with you.* Base encroacher! Is this the design of your flattering speeches? Far as matters have gone, I will for ever renounce you. You have an odious heart. Let me go, I tell you.

I was forced to obey, and she flung from me, repeating *base* and adding *flattering*, encroacher.

—Samuel Richardson, *Clarissa*

Here's the Beef

It was nothing but old meat.

—Schandorph, Description of a kiss in *Skovfogedbörnene*

 # 2. Games and Merriment

Oh, they sudden up and rise and dance;
Then sit again, and sigh, and glance;
Then dance again, and kiss.

—Sir John Suckling, *Ballad of a Wedding*

Who's Game for Kissing?

When the Welsh decided to have fun, they *really* had fun. An ancient law of theirs permitted kissing only at public games, such as "rope playing" or liquor-drinking festivities.

Play It Again, Kid

The Kirghiz youth of Central Asia played a game in which a boy enamored of a particular girl would, in her presence, sing a song or enact a difficult feat. The girl would stand in judgment of his performance and, if she approved, would reward him with a kiss.

A Kisser's Dozen

An English game, often played on holidays, allowed the ladies the initiative to choose the fellow she wished to be kissed by.

The players would first form a revolving circle. Any girl who so desired would break away from the ring and put a chip or handkerchief in the hand of one of the men. She would then run off, with the fellow—she hoped—in hot pursuit. Once caught, the girl was hauled back to the center of the ring and, before everyone, kissed twelve times in succession.

A similar game was called Hunt the Squirrel. The only difference was that, if the woman turned to face her pursuer in midflight, the roles would be automatically reversed and *she* would chase after *him*. Once one or the other was caught, the two would perform a series of dance steps called setting and then kiss.

The Hindu Lip-Locker

Lovers . . . play a kissing game in which they wager with each other as to which one will catch hold of the lips of the other first. When the woman loses, she pretends to cry and ask for a return match. When she loses a second time, she appears very much distressed and waits her chance until her lover is off his guard or asleep. Then she gets hold of his lower lip and holds it tight with her teeth until he is well aware of the fact that his lip is in a vise. After that she entrances him by moving her eyes and joking about their encounter. . . . Whatever things may be done by one of the lovers to the other, the same should be returned by the other, that is, if the woman kisses him, he should kiss her in return, if she strikes him, he should strike her in return.

—Dr. Edwin W. Hirsch, *The Power of Love*

The Revenge

Coaxed by the refreshing billows,
To the shore all maidens flock
And among the bushes hiding
Waits a youth the girls to shock.

Kiss the picture and you will see the man and woman kiss each other.

And no eye discerns the danger,
And no tongue by it is tied,
And the crowd in gleeful playing
Know of nothing yet to hide.

Say they: "Think if some one heard us;
Think if some one saw our sport!"
"Think if trees had ears to hear with!"
Says the youth in stepping forth.

"Chase him, catch him!" Well, already
He is caught before he has fled.
"Tie him, punish him!" And now he
To his penalty is led.

And what was the chain that bound him?
Bonds of flowers they on him laid.
And the punishment? A kiss of
Each and every handsome maid.

—Finnish poem

Deal Me a Kiss

In the Old West kisses were regularly employed in the game of whist. When a certain sequence of cards was arrived at, that player had the option of requesting a kiss from the dealer. The word "option" is stressed, of course, since players and dealers of the same sex were frequently not tickled over the idea of exchanging anything more intimate than a hearty handshake.

The Olympics Ignored This One

Kissing contests between young boys were frequently a part of ancient Greek games. According to the writings of Theocritus, kissing matches would be held in honor of Diocles, a Greek hero. Boys would assemble around Diocles' tomb "and he who most sweetly presses lip upon lip, returns laden with garlands to his mother."

Passing Kisses Between Laws

Among the nineteenth-century Washington elite, the Kiss Quadrille was a popular square dance at various government parties and balls. As described at that time in *The Rocky Mountain News*, "when it comes to 'swinging corners' each gentleman kisses his partner, and very delightful it must be." But, the newspaper wondered, "In the mad mazes of the political dance . . . are members of Congress to kiss each other?"

The Kiss Quadrille was practiced by "ordinary folk" as well, but they called it, much more simply, Smooch and Swing.

Dauncing oop Aye Kysse

. . . What foole would daunce
If that when daunce is doone,
He may not have at ladyes lips
That which in daunce he woon.

—Lovel, *Use and Abuse of Dauncing*

Whooping It Up

Humans are sometimes not very different from the whooping crane, who performs a dance prior to mating.

During the Elizabethan age, May Day celebrations featured dances about the Maypole, of which Philip Stubbes, in his *Anatomy of Abuses*, commented: ". . . what kissing and bussing, what smooching and slabbering one of another, what filthy groping and unclean handling is not practised in these dances?"

A popular pastime among fifteenth-century Italians and Spaniards was the "basse danse." Men dressed in skintight hose and pointed shoes and women wearing high, pointed hats would frequently exchange kisses

during all the moving about. One Italian dancer said that the planting of kisses was "bellisima for the lady in every measure of the dance, provided that she goes with swaying and undulating movements of the body in the manner prescribed." In one particular dance, *La Mercantia*, a single woman would hoof it with as many as five different men at once, bestowing kisses on each of them.

An eyewitness account of an aristocratic ball in 1580 Augsburg noted that women would sit in rows along a ballroom wall until a man approached, bowed, and kissed her hand. The woman then stood, the man took hold of her by the waist, then kissed her on the mouth. Sometimes they even danced.

As of the sixteenth century, it had become a regular custom in England for a woman to kiss her partner by the end of a dance. The men, reported *The Spectator*, "are obliged to dwell about a minute on the fair one's lips, or they will be too quick for the music, and dance quite out of time." The kissing that results from dancing, noted the *Minerva* in 1796, "operates as silent eloquence upon the hearts of men."

Some of the dances became rather daring, however, as men freely lifted women's skirts, squeezed their bosoms, and kissed in unbridled passion. It was said that, in performing the saraband, a sixteenth century Central American dance, "the breasts knock together [and] the hips sway . . . in a thousand positions [as] they close their eyes and dance the kiss." The saraband was considered so indecent that a Spanish law was passed in 1583 to keep people from humming the music to which it was danced.

Kissing dances are really quite tame when compared to earlier modes of dance. Originally, ancient tribes—from the Tahitians to the South American Puri—performed erotic dances that indeed culminated in full sexual intercourse.

Which brings us back to the whooping crane. For all its wild mating dances, the poor bird is threatening to become extinct. Maybe somebody should invite it to a screening of *Staying Alive*; a few tips from John Travolta couldn't hurt.

Naked Bush Bears No Kisses

The custom of kissing under the mistletoe was at one time adapted to a game in which one kiss was allowed for every berry on the bush. Pull off a berry, get a kiss. Once the mistletoe was bare, everyone had to stop kissing.

Playing for Kisses

> My love and I for kisses play'd;
> She would keep stakes; I was content;
> But when I won, she would be paid;
> This made me ask her what she meant.
> Pray, since see (quoth she) your wrangling vain,
> Take your own kisses; give me mine again.
> —William Strode
> "My Love and I for Kisses Play'd"

3. Lights! Camera! Kisses!

"I'm not directing this damn thing. God is!"
—Director Clarence Brown, during the filming
of the Greta Garbo–John Gilbert kissing
scene in *Flesh and the Devil* (MGM, 1925)

Where There's a Kiss, There's a Way

"Lustful and open-mouth kissing" was barred from Hollywood film productions in 1930 with the establishment of the Hays Production Code. A backlash response to a number of tinsel-town scandals, it provided the industry with a set of rules by which movies would reflect a given moral standard.

Few filmmakers were enamored of these restrictions, and Alfred Hitchcock was no exception. He ran up against the Code while filming *Notorious* in 1946. The length of a kiss was not permitted to exceed several seconds, yet Hitch had in mind a very long kissing scene between Cary Grant and Ingrid Bergman. How did he pull it off? By chopping up the kiss into a multitude of smacks, pecks, smooches, busses, and

nuzzles. A constant stream of interrupted kisses carried his two stars along a balcony, across a room, and through an entire telephone conversation. And the censors were powerless to do anything about it.

Kiss and Swell

Judge Manuel Morales of Brazil made a public attack on screen kisses in 1981. As part of a milestone ruling banning all public kissing, Morales took particular issue with "the cinematographic kiss, in which salivas mix to simply swell the sensuality."

Many young people were of a different opinion, however, and 2,000 of them proved it by marching through the streets of Sorocaba, chanting, "Kiss! Kiss! Kiss!" before clashing with police.

Brazilian filmmakers were probably sympathetic to the prokissers' cause; their film industry has since produced—and exported to America—a number of critically acclaimed movies featuring *plenty* of "saliva-mixing," with extensive nudity to boot.

Voyeur Viewing Pleasure

A movie made in 1963 called *Kiss* is exactly that—pure kissing.

For fifty minutes, several men and women passionately kiss in stark black-and-white close-up. Made by Andy Warhol, the avante garde production features no titles, no credits, and no sound. What *is* included, however, are images of the film stock trailing out of the camera at each original reel change.

Warhol also made movies called *Suicide*, *Sleep*, and *Eat*—though not necessarily in that order.

Great Moments in TV Dialogue No. 1

"Why don't you go kiss a light socket, buster."
—Carol Wayne to Jack Cassidy
in "The Trouble With Temple" *I Spy* (NBC, 1966)

Where There's Smoke . . .

One of the funniest kisses in movie history occurs in Mike Nichols' 1967 film classic, *The Graduate*.

Anne Bancroft and Dustin Hoffman in *The Graduate*, 1967

In a suite in the Taft Hotel, young Benjamin Braddock (Dustin Hoffman) attempts to seduce an older woman, Mrs. Robinson (Anne Bancroft). As she puffs away on a cigarette, Ben awkwardly tries to initiate some foreplay. Not realizing that Mrs. Robinson has just taken a drag on her cigarette, Ben suddenly places his mouth against hers and holds it there in a prolonged kiss. No fireworks. Ben finally ends the kiss and turns away in dejection, while Mrs. Robinson—much to her relief—blows out a huge cloud of inhaled smoke.

The Kiss Sublime

The first kiss ever to grace a movie screen in India occurred between actor Shashi Kapoor and actress Zeenat Aman in the 1978 Indian film, *Love Sublime*. The result of new film guidelines, the movie's landmark kiss nonetheless triggered a nationwide debate over censorship. Movie kisses had previously been banned in India, a 1928 study having determined that "ladies turn their heads away" during such scenes.

Kapoor insisted that the new creative freedom would only add logic to Indian love stories and even result in less cinema violence. M. G. Ramachandran, chief minister of the Indian state of Tamil Nadu (and part-time movie actor), labeled the Kapoor-Aman kissing sequences "an insult" and called for a mass protest.

The Kiss That Unclasps?

The kiss, in a motion picture, in close-up, impresses one as even more repellent than the showing of the sexual act. Lovers, sitting next to each other and watching such things from orchestra seats, will in embarrassment unclasp their hands.

—Emil Ludwig, *Of Life and Love*

Framed

In his *Movie Facts and Feats*, Patrick Robertson unearthed a unique tale that proves that cinema indeed has the power to alter the course of our personal lives.

In 1906, Marie Balteano agreed to marry the womanizing Prince Bengesco of Romania, provided he was faithful to her for two years prior to the wedding. The prince agreed.

Only days before the planned betrothal, Bengesco took his fiancee to a movie in Bucharest. As luck would have it, a newsreel was being shown that included recent documentary footage of the prince—being welcomed to his army tent with the kiss of a celebrated prostitute.

Needless to say, Marie canceled the wedding. That's show biz. . . .

A Tradition You Can't Refuse

The old Mafia tradition of younger "family" members kissing the hands

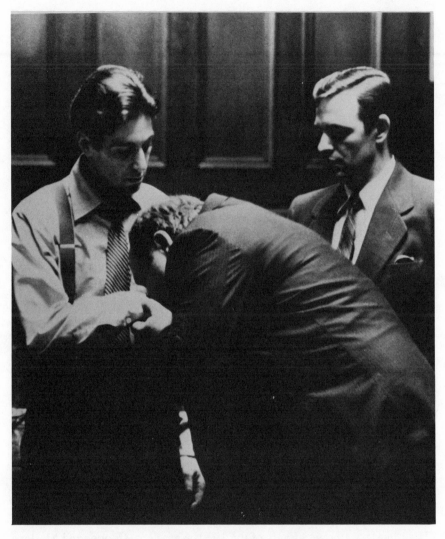

Al Pacino's hand is kissed in *The Godfather*, 1972.

of the older ones had fallen out of use in recent times—until *The Godfather* movies came out. There was such syndicate enthusiasm over the two motion pictures that the hand-kissing ritual was actually revived. A New Jersey undercover officer who'd infiltrated the mob told a Senate subcommittee in 1981 that many syndicate members had seen the films up to four times and were inspired enough by them to resurrect the kissing practice.

Great Moments in TV Dialogue No. 2

"Maggie, every time you kiss me like that, I know you're preparing me for something."

> —Gene Barry, in anticipation of being given a new assignment, in "The Man With the Power" *Amos Burke, Secret Agent* (ABC, 1965)

Dialing for Kisses

The ins and outs of kissing on television was one of the topics taught to acting students at Hollywood's Film Industry Workshop, an acting school established in 1962.

According to writer Peter Brown, director Tony Miller lectured one session: "You guys may be pros out on a date, but now you're going to share a kiss for the camera—and the camera alone. You'll find you don't know the first thing about it. . . . If you just settle down and smooch in bed it becomes a director's nightmare."

During a video session, Miller instructed a male student to put one of his fingers inside his acting partner's lips. "Her lips will flatten," said Miller, "and the camera will see flattering shadows. If you purse up your lips, those heavy smacking kisses will make you both look like guppies in an aquarium. The housewives at home will switch you off in favor of *Dialing for Dollars*."

Hollywood's Hardest

The "hardest" movie kissers of the 1930s were Gary Cooper and Marlene Dietrich, according to Wally Westmore, top Hollywood makeup artist.

Modus Operandi

In this cinema deliberately devised for arousing the spectator, mouths become greedy suction-cups clinging to male and female . . . the tongue diving in search of the tonsils.

> —Lo Duca and Bessy, *L'Érotisme au Cinema*

Deep Throats, Loose Lips, and Brass Knuckles

Actress Eleanor Parker's film debut occurred, sort of, in 1941 during the production of *They Died with Their Boots On*, a motion picture starring Errol Flynn and Olivia de Havilland. "I was very new at Warners," Parker later recalled, "and was visiting the *Boots* set one day. The director decided he needed a young thing to kiss Gig Young off to war, so I was drafted to do it. People who look for me in it can't find me for the very good reason that I was cut out of the final print." A rumor had it that the scene was dropped because a false mustache worn by Young got stuck to Parker's lip during the kiss.

Ms. de Havilland had her own kissing problems, but those were with Richard Burton on another movie, *My Cousin Rachel* (Fox, 1952). "The first time he grabbed me on the staircase," she recalled, "that was no stage kiss. He had his tongue down my mouth right there in front of the camera."

Kathryn Grayson reportedly had that problem with Mario Lanza, who not only "kept trying to stuff his tongue down my throat," she recalled, but "kept eating garlic for lunch." During filming of *The Toast of New Orleans* (MGM, 1950), Grayson had her costumer sew some brass bits into her gloves. "I socked him the next time he tried it," she said. "We never had any trouble after that."

The Future of the Kiss

Could six thousand people experience, all at once, the rapture of the very same kiss?

An image immediately comes to mind of masses of people crowding a football field, each person struggling to connect his or her lips to 5,999 other pairs of lips in a single, slobbering smooch. Though I don't believe it's ever actually been tried, the laws of the universe would certainly guarantee failure.

In his novel *Brave New World*, Aldous Huxley wrote of a future in which movie audiences could experience, together, the very smells, emotions, and tactile sensations that are enjoyed by the actors on the screen. By touching a pair of "feelies"—metal knobs affixed to one's theater seat—a movie viewer could indeed experience a movie with each of his senses.

When Huxley's screen actors kiss, their "stereoscopic lips" cause the feelies to titillate the "facial erogenous zones of the six thousand spectators," causing them to "tingle with almost intolerable pleasure."

If moviemakers of today can simulate earthquakes, you'd think they could present a love story in *Smoocharound*. It would be a *much* more pleasant way to feel the ground beneath you tremble. And who knows—it might even solve the problem of not having a date to take to the movies on Saturday night.

The essence of Huxley's Kiss-of-the-Future fits neatly into Marshall McLuhan's Global Village and today's computerized patch-me-in-and-punch-me-up society.

But kissing is kissing, and no amount of high technology will ever be able to improve on it—whether inside a movie theater, parked car or doorway.

One kiss more, and so farewell.

—Anonymous, *Loyal Garland*

Credits

Grateful acknowledgment is made to the following people and organizations for granting permission to reprint material in this book:

By permission of the Associated Press: "Kiss and *Don't* Make Up." Reprinted from *Literary Anecdotes* by Edwin Fuller, courtesy of the Crown Publishing Group: "That's Why He's a Colonel"; "The Most-Kissed War Hero"; "Art Imitates Life—Sometimes"; "The Case of the Mysterious Visitor." Quotations reprinted by permission of Peter Brown, Washington, D.C.: "Dialing for Kisses." Reprinted with permission of Macmillan Publishing Company from *THE SHRINKING ORCHESTRA* by William Wood. © William Wood, 1963: "People Are Funny."

The illustrations in this book, noted by page number, are used with the express permission of the sources listed.
11, 142. Acme/International/Lou Hutt.
15. Mary Evans Picture Library.
16, 17, 118, 119, 124, 125. MOMMA by Mell Lazarus. Courtesy of Mell Lazarus and Field Newspaper Syndicate.
33. Courtesy of Mel Calman.
37. United Artists Corp.
44. Metro-Goldwyn-Mayer.
45. Universal Pictures.
47. From *The Underground Sketch Book* of Tomi Ungerer. Copyright © by Tomi Ungerer.
52, 73. Drawing by Marcus Hamilton reprinted with his permission.
55. European/Acme.
74. Vitascope.
86. From *The Female Approach* by Ronald Searle. MacDonald: London, 1950.
103. Drawing by Geo. Price; Copyright © 1976 The New Yorker Magazine, Inc.
136. Copyright © 1979 by Village of Deerfield, Illinois.
138. Columbia Pictures.
157. Courtesy of the Elbee Company, San Antonio, Texas.
161. Richard Erdoes.
163. Avco Embassy Pictures Corp.
165. Paramount Pictures.

Index

Of Human Bondage, 154
O. Henry, 149
Oldoini, Nicchia, 78
Oliver, Susan, 132
Origin(s) of kissing, 18–22, 33
Otho (emperor of Rome), 109–10
Ovid, 36, 50, 75, 151

Pacino, Al, 165
Pajama Game, The, 120
Parker, Eleanor, 167
Parsons, Louella, 90–91
Patmore, Coventry, 87
Paul VI (pope), 113
Peele, George, 124
Perry Mason, 123–24
Petacci, Clara, 118
Peter the Great, 50
Phelps, Marion, 11
Pickford, Mary, 122
Plato, 32
Plautus, 36
Plong, Carl, 64
Pound, Ezra, 77
Powers, Dave, 143
Private Benjamin, 69
Prouty, Rex, 12
Puberty, 95
Puck, 87–88

Rachevskaya, Tania, 145
Ramachandran, M.G., 164
Ray, John, 36
Reade, Charles, 45–46
Reap the Wild Wind, 54
Redford, Robert, 128
Restif de la Bretonne, N.E., 63
Rice, John C., 74
Richardson, Samuel, 154–55
Rigg, Diana, 107–8
Robertson, Patrick, 137, 164
Rodin, Auguste, 49, 88
Rogers, Gary, 127
Rogers, Roy, 92
Rollo the Ganger, 112
Rome, 97
Rome, ancient, 23, 82, 96, 101–2, 107, 109–10
Roosevelt, Eleanor, 41
Rostand, Edmond, 13, 17
Rousseau, Jean-Jaques, 151
Rowland, Helen, 71
Rudolf (of Hapsburg), 108
Runeberg, Johan L., 29–30, 71
Russia, 98, 133

Sadat, Anwar, 122
St. Denis, Ruth, 49

Sale of kisses, 127–28
Saliva, 106, 116–17
Saxe, John G., 127, 131
Schandorph, 155
Schlesinger, Arthur J., 112
Schnitzler, Arthur, 66
Scholasticus, Agathias, 39
Scott, Walter, 129
Secundus, Johannes, 51
Shakespeare, William, 23, 41, 43, 52, 54, 58, 63, 112, 131, 147
Sharks, 118
Shaw, H.W. See Billings, Josh
Shelley, Percy Bysshe, 31–32
Sheridan, Richard B., 84
Siegfried, 56
Signals, 80–81, 83
"Sleeping Beauty," 92
Smith, Horace and James, 93
Smuggling, 81, 127
Social kissing, 93–96
Socrates, 114
Some Like It Hot, 126
Soritch, A., 133
Sound of kisses, 57–59
Speakes, Larry, 110–11
Spit, 106, 116–17
Stedman, E.C., 72
Steele, Richard, 18
Stevenson, Connally D., 109
Stolen kisses, 83–88
Stone, Herbert, 74
Strode, William, 160
Stuart, Gilbert, 78–79
Stubbs, Philip, 158–60
Subway tokens, 126
Suckling, John, 155
Summersby, Kay, 77
Sunday, Bloody Sunday, 111
Superstitions, 99–106
Suzuki, Kazuo, 80
Swift, Jonathan, 18
Swinburne, Algernon, 49

Taylor, Estelle, 65, 70
Teasdale, Sarah, 68
Television kisses, 162
See also specific TV series
Tennyson, Alfred Lord, 55, 68
That Hamilton Woman, 56
They Died with Their Boots On, 167
Throwing kisses, 68, 93, 94, 109–10
Toast of New Orleans, The, 167
To Have and Have Not, 38
Toomey, Regis, 56
Trevillion, Paul, 65
Trigger (horse), 68
Turgenev, Ivan, 113, 150